This may be *[...]*
issues. Reid *[...]*
out, he knows *people* with all their fears and foibles
but more importantly he knows God. If speaking to
yourself is the first sign of madness then this book has
exposed me! I constantly found myself speaking out
loud to this book saying, 'yes' or 'amazing'. I also
admit that on more than one occasion I was silenced
as I saw my own sin and character defects described
on the page. I was impressed by the honesty of this
book which reflects and dare I say it, even improves
on Spurgeon's 'Lectures to my students'!

Reid Ferguson believes that a congregation will
rise to the level on a pastor's passion and love for
Christ. I have no doubt that this book will help to
raise the bar as we are inspired to love Christ more.
This book has a great emphasis as reflected in Reid's
advice, 'Be with God, Be with God'.

David Meredith
Culloden Free Church, Inverness, Scotland

'The Pastor's Little Book' is not about homiletics or
the craft of constructing a sermon; it is not even about
pastoral ethics per se. This book is about many of the
gray areas of ministry. Written in the style of a
devotional, it is a compilation of pithy and stark
aphorisms that come straight from the trenches. There
is humor as Ferguson describes the parade of
personalities that circulate through our churches. Even
as he elaborates on contending with some of these
rather difficult and trying personalities, it is never with
disrespect, disdain or bitterness. In all that the author
says the compassion of the pastor's heart is evident in
every thought.

Let us hear what it says as we continue to examine
ourselves and serve God's people with gladness.

Ken Jones
Alliance of Confessing Evangelicals

Reid Ferguson blends common sense and uncommonly mature biblical wisdom in this helpful handbook for church leaders. He is refreshingly candid, consistently thought-provoking, and eminently practical. Every pastor, young and old, will recognize the pitfalls and problems Reid offers help for. His advice is seasoned and sound, the fruit of a lifetime lived in the parsonage—first under his father's ministry; now in his own. Pastors at every stage of their ministry will find this book a wealthy resource. And for the young pastor just entering the ministry, it is indispensable.

Phillip R. Johnson
Executive Director, Grace to You Ministries

If the best 'little books' are pithy enough to make you reflect and grow spiritually, this is one of the best Little Books. Don't be deceived by the light touch. We all regularly need recalling to the self forgetfulness that Reid Ferguson inculcates, to the humble recognition that the congregation is Christ's and not ours. As we journey to ministry, we shall meet the people, and be in the marriages, he mirrors back to us. When we are dispirited; when we feel unappreciated, opposed or unsupported; the wisest responses can be considered from these pages. Read a chapter every week!

C. Peter White
Sandyford Henderson Memorial Church
Glasgow, Scotland

Reid Ferguson writes of what he knows: that the pastoral ministry is not for the faint of heart. With an abundance of wisdom, he is rooted in Scripture and grounded in reality. Pastors and parishioners alike will profit from the time spent reading this necessary work.

Dr. Don Kistler
President, Soli Deo Gloria Ministries

The Little Book
of Things You Should
Know About Ministry

By Reid Ferguson

Christian Focus

Reformation & Revival Ministries

ISBN 1-85792-786-9

© Copyright Reid A.Ferguson

Published in 2002
by
Christian Focus Publications, Ltd.
Geanies House, Fearn, Tain,
Ross-shire, IV20 1TW, Great Britain.
and
Reformation & Revival Ministries
P.O. Box 88216
Carol Stream, Illinois, 60188 USA

Printed and bound by
Cox & Wyman, Ltd. Reading, Berkshire
Typeset in Plantin

Cover Design by Alister MacInnes

Contents

Foreword
John H. Armstrong

_____

The late A. W. Tozer once said: "The ministry is one of the most perilous professions." I doubt that members of your church can relate to such a statement.

Misunderstandings about the role and responsibilities of ministers abound in our age. Formal education taught most of us in the gospel ministry many valuable lessons. We learned how to interpret the Scriptures wisely before we entered upon this work. We also learned the essential core of orthodoxy so we could teach and protect the faith in public and in private. Gaining the necessary tools for our ministry was essential. Though some think otherwise, decrying intellectual pursuit as a waste of time, it is essential that a minister be "trained in the words of the faith and of good doctrine" (1 Timothy 4:6). We must have _this_ training, regardless of how we get it. It may come in formal or informal ways but make no mistake about it, training is necessary for _good_ ministry.

There are voices today that insist anyone can do pastoral ministry, so long as they "feel called." I would not decry a true "call" to the ministry for one moment. Without it you will not survive in this demanding work. But you must have more. A calling merely points you in the right direction. "Training in godliness" necessarily takes time.

The proverb is correctly applied here that it is the "little foxes that spoil the vine." Fruitful ministry comes over the long haul because ministers keep a wise and careful "self watch." Those who do this will continually seek help for their holy work. *The Little Book of Things You Should Know About Ministry* is a book I welcome precisely because it will help the modern pastor better understand and cope with the "little foxes" of the Christian ministry.

The biblical pastor is first and foremost a spiritual mentor and then a shepherd of souls. I submit to you that modern pastors, at least in the West, often become very good managers. The better they manage the church the larger their circle of influence becomes. We then make our managers into messiahs. The daily work of ministry, in our modern context, is usually about tasks, plans, and job descriptions. But we are not called to be managers. We are called to shepherd sheep. We do this best by feeding and leading, which is the true work of spiritual direction.

Eugene Peterson, warning against the two common models of ministry that we adopt, calls them the managerial and the messianic. He suggests that we easily adopt the messianic role when we major on serving and helping people in trouble. Understanding and mercy are common to most of us in ministry. As we care for people they sense a greater need for us to be their ministers. Somewhere along the way we cross a line when, as Peterson suggests, "my messianic work takes center stage and Messiah is pushed to the sidelines." The sheep need us and we begin to feel our importance. In our eagerness to fulfill this role we can actually hinder their growth, both spiritually and emotionally.

We slip into the managerial role when we sense that our people need us to guide and lead them if they are to grow. Says Peterson, "I am responsible for the successful operation of a religious organization—if I am going to do this well, I am going to have to get the best help available, and deploy the forces strategically." This leads ministers to seek for the "best" leaders in the flock, those who are gifted and who can create a good impression. The minister is in a good place to see the gifts of the flock and thus to challenge the people. Peterson adds, "As I get people working with me, my image is enhanced. And in the course of doing this I cross a line: what started out as managing people gift's for the work of the kingdom of God becomes the manipulation of people's lives for the building up of my pastoral ego."

Peterson wisely adds that the "tough part" (at least in this culture) is to develop the skill of slipping quite effortlessly in and out of the messianic and managerial roles. For sure, we must do both these works but we should understand that they are the high profile works of ministry. What about the small things? What about the day-to-day realities that make us good spiritual mentors, spiritual directors who can quietly move people toward the Savior though our labors? Peterson concludes: "Spiritual direction is practiced by pastors in the very context that constantly interferes with the practice. This is why it is so infrequently practiced: the setting is not congenial."

Now here is the real challenge. Peterson concludes that "spiritual direction [is] what I am doing when I do not think I am doing anything important." I like that. It is what I have come to understand first-hand after thirty-plus years in the ministry. How can I pay attention to the spiritual graces of a faithful ministry while not putting too much emphasis upon my personal skills to help, i.e., to become a messiah to my people? How can I lead my church, in the power of the Spirit, without the real issue becoming my personal management style and giftedness?

Reid Ferguson grew up in the home of a wise and faithful pastor. He has a keen practical and penetrating insight into the nature of pastoral work. He has learned some simple lessons in his own ministry that will profoundly serve his fellow ministers. He writes lucidly. He understands the great traditions of spiritual ministry but he is practically rooted in present realities.

Here you will find help to deal with real church issues like "special interest groups." Here you will also be challenged to drop a number of mistaken notions that you have picked up along the way. And you will certainly learn some practical things about avoiding needless controversies, which all too often destroy long term pastoral ministry. Since ministry is two parts godliness and one part humor you will also be urged to laugh.

A. W. Tozer once noted that, "Whatever is getting the attention from our spiritual leaders is what we finally come to accept as orthodoxy in any given period of history." If this is true I submit that the modern ministry desperately needs a new reformation, one that reshapes and retools the way we see our work and the way we follow our Chief Shepherd in it. Reid

Ferguson understands this need for reformation in ministry. In short, Ferguson understands that it is the "little foxes" that often destroy our work. In this excellent book he provides some basic things that all ministers need to think about more clearly and act upon more faithfully. This is a wise little book.

John H. Armstrong,
Reformation & Revival Ministries

Preface

Moses Hadas once wrote a review of a book which read: "This book fills a much needed gap on my bookshelf." He had a way with words. It is my sincere hope that this little book will do just the opposite of the one Hadas cited; that it will fill a sore gap on your bookshelf.

There are, in my estimation, three books which speak directly to pastoral work which no man who endeavors to preach should ever be without: C.H. Spurgeon's *Lectures to My Students*; D. Martyn Lloyd-Jones' *Preachers and Preaching*; and Richard Baxter's *The Reformed Pastor*. Spurgeon's work I recommend to be read once a year. Spurgeon himself had his dear wife read him Baxter's book regularly after he retired from preaching on the Lord's Day. And Jones' book equips the preacher, so that he may better pastor – since our first contribution toward the spiritual health of our people is to feed them upon God's own Word.

Each of these works speak so eloquently and powerfully to the preacher's needs, that little can be said to improve upon them. And yet, it is this writer's experience that there are some select things which no one ever says to the pastor about his work and himself which would be of great usefulness if brought to the fore. Perhaps I might even be able to spare you some of the pain, heartache and foolish mistakes that I have already made. That is my desire – to add just a little more to the equipping you've already had.

I want to make it clear that much of what you will read here is not simply the fruit of dispassionate observation, but lessons learned in the aftermath of my own grave errors. A precious trust has been committed into our hands by our being allowed the privilege of building into peoples' lives upon the foundation of Christ that has already been laid. If you are anything like me, it can be a very easy thing to be a raging bull in the china shop of men's souls. We minister to peers, not underlings. We too are sheep. Sheep under-shepherding other sheep to be sure, but sheep nonetheless. It is my sincere hope that the chapters below will help you avoid some of those errors to which I have been prone, both for you own sake as well as for those you faithfully tend.

In many cases, it will be abundantly apparent that the topics addressed could use much more "in depth" treatment. That will have to wait for another day, and perhaps, other contributors. The object here is not to treat each of these exhaustively (this author is certainly not qualified to do so anyway), but more to call them to the mind's attention – and to give each reader room to think them through more carefully in their own context. Thus there is much contained herein which is broad and general rather than precise and specific. That is by design. Keeping the chapters short and thought provoking, while calling certain central ideas to the fore will (I hope) both keep the reader's attention, and prevent them from being bogged down in applicational detail which might hinder the practical use intended. One might look at some of them as slightly expanded proverbs.

If the subjects seem to jump erratically, it is because I am filling holes, not creating a smooth pavement. Bear with me. If you think I left something out, it is probably in one of the three books mentioned above. Even at that, there is some overlap with them. But I have tried to avoid that, and just leave you with some critical material. May God be pleased to bless it and use it for His glory.

One last thought: as I began to commit these thoughts to paper, it occurred to me that just tossing some of these things into your collective laps may be somewhat sterile in and of itself. I would recommend that if you have picked up this copy of the book, it might be wise to find another brother at least – if not a few others - with whom you can discuss the various concepts tendered, in an atmosphere where you can work through specific applications prayerfully and peer to peer. If you cannot do that – please feel free to contact me personally if I can be of any assistance. We are all co-laborers here. If we can help one another in the task committed to us, I believe we will be better Shepherds. To that end, letters may be sent to me care of the Evangelical Church of Fairport, 38 E. Church St., Fairport NY 14450. Or I can be e-mailed at reid@reformed.org. No Shepherd should be without access to a least one other who is laboring in the same field.

One

The Seductive Power of Novelty

Acts 17:21 – "Now all the Athenians and the strangers visiting there used to spend their time in nothing other than telling or hearing something new."

Never underestimate the seductive power of novelty. Both you and the people you are called to under-Shepherd on behalf of Christ are susceptible to it. Novelty comes in all shapes and forms: dazzling dainties that catch the eye, intrigue the mind, delight the senses and titillate our curiosity; novelty in doctrine, in the form of Christian fads, movements, trends, etc. Novelty may be brought in by others, and may sometimes even arise out of your own study as you seek to be original, thought provoking and stimulating to your flock.

Even though some novelty may have served to bring a new and necessary emphasis upon something lacking in the Church at times, it must always be analyzed, contexualized and utilized by the norms established in Scripture. The Charismatic move is one example that can serve us well in this regard. Can there be anything inherently wrong in turning people's attention toward living more consciously dependent upon the indwelling Spirit of God? And yet look at the abuses, wrong-headedness and subjectivism which also flowed from it. One certainly cannot blame the Spirit of God, nor the Word, nor the many who genuinely found the renewal of such deliberate dependence both vital, and worth spreading. But caution must always be exercised.

Current trends should neither define the nature of our preaching and work within the Church, nor are they to be wholly ignored. We need to know what the current buzz is so that we can warn and protect – when necessary – pointedly. But bandwagons are awfully seductive. The noise and color and flurry of life that surrounds celebratory cavalcades can have us marching in step with the latest *zeitgeist* before we know it. We pick up the peculiar language of the trend almost unconsciously. We like sounding informed, "with it", and cutting edge. The glint in folk's eyes when we toss around the familiar nomenclature provides us with a subtle reinforcement that feeds our nearly unconscious desire for tacit approval. It is a trap – a very dangerous one. And like the Athenians, it is one which the modern Church and its pastors fall into regularly.

Now novelty appeals to people principally on two heads: 1 – the simple charm of cleverness; and 2 – the pride of exclusivity. Both of these inducements are far more powerful than we might imagine.

The simple charm of cleverness, the power of well-turned phrases, catchwords or a slightly new spin on an old doctrine to quickly become entrenched, spread and accepted as normative truth is unfathomable. Just as people love to watch sleight of hand tricks time after time after time – even though they know there is a trick behind it – the sheer delight of having the senses tantalized by the visual effect of something we know cannot happen is mesmerizing. It is just the same with truth. We can truly know deep down that what we are hearing is not in line with what we know to be the established norms of biblical truth, and yet the mind is caught by the charm of what seems to be what cannot be. And we are hooked – not as much by the raw idea itself, as by the inner tension the new thought brings. It is like going back to ride a roller coaster again, when we know it is going to churn our stomachs. That churning which would be so disturbing as to bring panic in a normal situation – say on the highway – is great fun in the controlled environment of the amusement park.

Mark it well however, when the root idea or doctrine is finally exposed by someone who in clear-headedness points it out to us, we are typically more upset at being robbed of the tantalization we enjoyed, than we are that someone else in fact deceived us. Remember this when approaching those who you seek to disabuse of such wrong notions. Often, they respond not with gratitude at being awakened from the spell, but are rather annoyed that their pleasant dream has been disturbed, and their fanciful new bauble has been stripped of its value as it has been exposed as nothing but paste.

An example of the above can be seen in something as commonplace as the advent of the phrase "the Lord helps those who help themselves." Now the phrase itself does contain a modicum of truth. One could, without doing violent harm to the text, apply it to Paul's admonition in 2 Thessalonians 3:10, "For even when we were with you, we used to give you this order: if anyone is not willing to work, then he is not to eat, either." It would not be improper to note that God has certainly made provision for His people, and that in drawing upon the resources given to the Church to supply genuine needs, we must be good stewards of those resources. Hence, we might be called upon to supply food to one who is without. Yet, so that men learn to labor as is proper, and so that the resources of the local congregation are not unnecessarily taxed – we should be careful not to help freeloaders. In this case, God's provision to help is tied to the willingness of the one in need to also help themselves by laboring. The problem is that what gains universal acceptance in the first place – such as this type of maxim, soon, by virtue of its widespread acceptance – also gains universal application. This is a very great danger. So it is that George Barna can point out in one survey he conducted, that "four out of five born again Christians" believe that "God helps those who help themselves" is an accurate statement. Beyond that, 34 per cent of Evangelicals believe that the statement comes from the Bible (as do 31 per cent of Roman Catholics and an equal percentage of those in mainline denominations), and the vast majority of those believe it has a direct bearing on the doctrine of salvation.

In the second place, such novelties find quick shelter in the bosoms of men because they play into our prideful, wicked desire to be thought of – by others as well as ourselves – as unique. And little can so quickly gratify this lust as being one who has laid hold of some seductively crafted nuance of Scripture, or a viewpoint which sets us apart from the rest. "Bread eaten in secret is pleasant" (Proverbs 9:17b).

Ancient Gnosticism was a fierce enemy of the Church because of this very seduction. When men believe they possess some secret knowledge, some unique and special insight or framework, they become terrors to themselves and others. When we as ministers of the gospel fall into this trap, woe unto to those committed to our charge! When once indulged in, this cancer of the soul will lead us to make our congregations to separate from all others based upon our pet doctrinal spin. We will spoil them for the Body of Christ at large. We will make them wary of any who do not hold our view and prideful against the rest who do not share our insight. It will make our congregations spiritually incestuous and cultic. We will set ourselves up like little authoritarian dictators over our doctrinal banana republics. This is a very great evil among the brethren and we must guard against it in ourselves, and in others. Where the "jealousy and selfish ambition" exist that make these things so attractive to us, we must also expect them to be accompanied by "disorder and every evil thing" (James 3:16).

Wed these two things together, our quick delight with the clever and our inward desire toward the recognition of exclusivity, and we have twin terrors of unmentionable havoc to reckon with.

What will serve us best in these cases is to be often reminded of that admonition of Paul's in the second letter to the Corinthians – "But I am afraid that, as the serpent deceived Eve by his craftiness, your minds will be led astray from the simplicity and purity of devotion to Christ" (2 Cor. 11:3). Oh the evil that prevails, because we will not content ourselves with the "simplicity and purity of devotion to Christ."

Nothing is good, simply because it is new. Its novelty is not a recommendation. Test everything by Scripture. Not just in mere content, but in application. It is quite true that Elijah made the axe head float. So what?

Two

Special Interest Groups

─────────────────────────────

1 Corinthians 14:26 : "What is the outcome then, brethren? When you assemble, each one has a psalm, has a teaching, has a revelation, has a tongue, has an interpretation. Let all things be done for edification."

The local church is often host to a cadre of special interest groups within it. The object of listing these "Special Interest Groups" as I have below, is not to denigrate any. It is simply to alert the mind to their existence and their operations. These are not criticisms of people, but merely observations regarding the emphases or bent of some, so that you are not surprised when you encounter them. Nor do I mean to imply that everyone in your congregation will fall into one of these or any other such groups. That is in no wise the case, but it is helpful to recognize them, as then you can understand the questions behind the (loaded) questions you may be asked. Questions that come seemingly out of left field. It is not that they are trying to trap you per se, but are using their questions as a means of stating their view in a manner which makes the logic of it undeniable – at least to them. Now there are some general observations we need to make first.

Note that each of these groups has their own lobby and lobbyist. It is generally one who represents him or herself and usually a very small faction of sympathizers. Most often, they are very sincere. Usually, they have a well developed biblical argument for their view, albeit a very narrow one. Each can contribute richly. Each can potentially do great harm. Each has a right to be heard. Without them, you have a church of apathetics – these speak because they care. Each seeks to motivate the church toward what they perceive as the common good.

It seems best to me to treat them each as consultants in their respective fields. In this manner, you can utilize their gifts for the body, but not swallow each perspective as a defining whole. This also lets you keep them in the local assembly, when often they tend to float. In that they are listened to, and their advice sought, we would hope that they will stick around long enough to mature past some of this short-sightedness and in a broader context be even more of a blessing to the congregation as a whole. Each one's "revelation," each one's "tongue," each one's "interpretation" must be handled so as to bring the maximum benefit to the body at large – not to them individually.

Let us make just a few comments on each for you to consider.

a. *Politists* – Specialists in Church GOVERNMENT. Typically they've scrutinized every evil of Presbyterianism versus Episcopalianism versus Congregationalism, and vice versa, with a deep knowledge of almost every misshapen form or combination of each imaginable. And they are not bashful about letting you know exactly which scheme the Holy Spirit codified for every church in every place to follow. No doubt they may even advance that the Kingdom is patterned after one or the other in Heaven as we speak. These are good folks to approach if you are looking to rewrite your constitution and by-laws for instance. They can save you many hours of running and research. Facts and figures, good points and bad points, and methods of implementation are generally at their fingertips. In Church disputes, they are usually spot-on in citing the

polity structure under which you labor. In
times of congregational instability they can be
wonderfully stabilizing, since they function
well under the notion of Lex Rex instead of
the "fly by the seat of the pants" of many
others. This can be a great weakness, but also
a great plus. Which one it will be will largely
be determined by how you deal with them.

b. *Programists* – Specialists in Church
PROGRAMS. Invariably, they have a great
idea they'd like YOU to implement. There
simply MUST be women's groups, single's
groups, married couple's groups, family
groups, Christian's with pets groups, men's
groups, children's groups, groups for people
who have yet to see the value of groups and
groups for people recovering from groups. Of
course, they are neither right nor wrong. The
problems for us are not in responding to what
might be the legitimate creation of some
particular group to meet a specific need within
our congregation. The problems lie in either
falling into the mistaken notion that anything
like a group which may be begun, must be
carried on to perpetuity: "Once a group,
forever an institution"; or, allowing ourselves
to be manipulated by the ubiquitously implied
(if not verbally expressed) – they want YOU to

do it; or, succumbing to the notion that "groups" are inherently necessary and always positive.

Sometimes, these folks are just bored. Sometimes program oriented people are trying to run away from home without leaving it, and the last thing they need is such a diversion. Another night out at the Church is just one more way to escape from dealing with real life at home. They need to be back home, loving their spouses and children, and pouring themselves into them. We need to remember that Scripture isn't as much concerned with making men, more manly men, or women more womanly women, as it is with making both men and women – godly.

Remember too, that there is no value in any program just for the sake of having a program. Programs ought most often to function like prescription medicines. They are to be constructed around real needs and only utilized until the condition is rectified. Then, they should be disposed of. Just because the previous pastor had "spiritual inventory" night once a month does not mean you must too. Then again, because he did nothing of the sort does not require that you should not. When there are specific deficiencies brought to your attention that demonstrate a real need which can be met by beginning some sort of group – call your programist, and get him or her working on it.

One more short word here. Pastors are often quite guilty of being slanted this way ourselves. And we will make short work of some excellent people if we too are always coming up with programs, notions and activities that we just delight in dumping into someone else's lap to accomplish. If you do not want to be the victim of being tagged to carry out everyone else's pet idea, you had better be prepared to treat them in like fashion. The pastorate is not the place where you get to play with all the kooky ideas that have filtered through your head over time, while making others miserable in the execution of them. If you have a burden for door-to-door evangelism, then YOU go door-to-door. When others are likewise burdened, they'll join you.

c. *Formists* – Specialists in styles of WORSHIP. This is a broad category. It involves those who have strong opinions on the use or disuse of creeds; Scripture reading; standing, sitting and kneeling (when, where and how); instrumental accompaniment or no; KJV only or other translations; times, number and days of services; liturgy or free-wheeling; one preacher or group participation; the evil of church buildings; the merits of cell groups; more expositional preaching; more felt-need response; fewer songs; more songs; shorter prayers; more prayer; ad infinitum ad nauseam. It will be occupied by everyone from those who want the light fixtures to sway and the windows to shatter each time the "Praise Band" (whatever THAT is) cranks it up, to exclusive Psalmodists, and everything in between.

On the more "contemporary" side, they will couch their arguments in terms of "freedom" and "liberty" in worship. They will be quick to point out that David appointed thousands of musicians, and that under Solomon they played loudly in a tiny, all metal interior Temple. On the other end of the spectrum, you'll be told that we can do nothing in the act of worship but what is specifically defined in Scripture. Both can build a pretty convincing Biblical argument, as most of the others in their various camps can. Listen to them all. Then structure your worship around the God and Christ you are worshipping in the manner that seems most fitting with His glory. Be more concerned with offering up something that is commensurate with His dignity, and let the Formists render their suggestions for how that can be done.

d. *Doctrinists* – Specialists in a species of pet DOCTRINE. These folks make themselves known very quickly. In the course of almost any conversation, on any topic, they will invariably find a way to bring it around to discussing doctrine "X". Preachers are often this way ourselves. So a good caution for us is to be found in examining them. If you find that every sermon ends up mentioning your favorite doctrinal stance, you may need to make some adjustments yourself. I believe it is G. Campbell Morgan who relates the story of one preacher who was a Baptist with a capital "B". Preaching from Genesis 3:9 on "Adam, where are you?"; he had the following as his points for the sermon: 1-where Adam was; 2-how Adam got there; 3-how God was seeking him; 4-a few words on the subject of baptism. If you are giving your congregation a healthy diet on the systematic exposition of the Scriptures, you will find yourself giving both balanced and nourishing meals. But they can be supplemented from time to time, and often doctrinists are good people for the job. Have your doctrinist present a short series (IF they can teach) on some midweek or Sunday evening services. All might benefit richly from the time and effort they've expended in their particular field of interest.

e. *Agendists* – Specialists in working for their private AGENDA or "color". Agendists can migrate. For this reason, it can be difficult to get a fix on them. They may join other special interest groups from time to time if they think that group is really onto something, or if it looks like that group's pursuit will dovetail with their own. Most often, what it is that they are really after is wanting the church to have a particular "feel". That may be something they can actually articulate in concrete terms, but I have found that rare. Typically, they are as ambiguous about what they really want in their own minds as they are in their expression of it to you. Do not drive yourself to distraction over it. You can no more allow each and every agenda to drive the Church than you can allow each member of the congregation to adjust the thermostat to their personal liking as they enter the building each Lord's Day.

f. *Activists* – Specialists in SOCIAL INVOLVEMENT. Activists make good deacons with some spiritual direction under

their belts. But the constant battle is to help
keep them from confounding mere social
ministrations with spirituality. Of course, the
same is true conversely. We need to keep
others from thinking that spiritual pursuits
are to be thought of as reason to ignore the
real, temporal needs of others. Spiritual men
and women should care about natural needs,
but they should also be able to understand
them as an outward expression of their
Christianity, not the sum and substance of it.
We must never forget that a freezing man
needs a coat as well as the gospel. Just as we
must never forget that having given him the
coat apart from the gospel only sends him to
Hell more comfortably. Activists are good
people to use to keep an eye out for others.
Sadly, these folks are also unusually prone to
gossip under the guise of "keeping everyone
up to date". This tendency must be watched
closely, and dealt with quickly and decisively
when it arises.

g. *Separatists* – Specialists in Christian
ISOLATION. We might also use terms like
Purists, Isolationists, Holyists, Solemnists. All
of these are simply slightly different approaches
to the same problem. Separatists work on one
basic theory – fear of contamination. No

matter how subtly it is expressed, or how orthodox their doctrinal framework may be, undergirding everything is the notion that sin is caught. Failure comes from exposure. Environment cures all. Of course, this comes from a faulty notion both of sin and redemption. If the theory of a pristine environment being the cure to sinning were true, then Adam and Eve would have never fallen. And if sin is something contracted by mere exposure, then Christ could not have remained pure. They may swear on a stack of Bibles that they believe in the preservation of the saints, but they live like they could be out the door tomorrow. They are Galatians, living on "touch not, taste not."

What these folks are stellar at however, is watching social trends. They know every new toy, kind of music, literature, TV program, and movie, and why it's bad. As the saying goes, just because a man is paranoid, it doesn't mean someone isn't after him. But these dear souls need to be delivered from the constant fear in which they live, for it often drives them to serious extremes, and extremes make for odd bedfellows. They are most likely to form home groups, without being under the auspices of any, including the Church. It is how cults and militia groups spring up. But we can take advantage of their keen ability to sniff and see and hear for things amiss. And sometimes they can spot things which we do very well to accept as sound warnings.

h. *Inclusionists* – Specialists in ECUMENISM. They march under the banner of "Anything goes, as long as you say Jesus." Their problem is the exact opposite of the Separatists. They have little or no discernment at all. If a Separatist has a swimming pool in his backyard, he builds a fence around it, locks the gate, keeps his kids in the house and tells them that they should never go near water because they will drown. The Inclusionist wouldn't dream of building a fence, leaves his doors and windows open all of the time, has never once warned his kids about the possibility of drowning, and lets his toddlers run around unsupervised. If BOTH of them would just teach their kids how to swim – we'd all be better off. But lack of balance in all of these tendencies is what it is we are combating.

Now the Inclusionist is as likely to consider Rush Limbaugh an Evangelical as he is to consider himself one. Mormons are just another denomination, not a cult. Dr Laura preaches the gospel as well as anyone else, and

anybody who says they are "born again", is.
They need to cultivate discernment. But at the
same time, they can serve to keep us all from
falling into the Separatist trap. They remind us
that the Church exists outside of our four walls;
outside of our denomination; outside of our
ethnic group; outside of our century; and even
in many cases – outside of our "faith tradition."
They are as great at ignoring sacred cows as
others are at worshipping them. They will make
you read books you would never buy. They will
keep you from waving a grandiose hand of
condemnation over everyone who has not yet
bent the knee to your own ministry.

i. *Frustrationists* – Specialists in theoretical
MINISTRY. Generally, this group is
populated by frustrated preachers and
teachers. And you will find huge repositories
of gold in these hills. Sadly, it is usually buried
beneath layers of disappointment, self-pity,
disillusionment and bitterness.

Often these are men with a discernable
measure of giftedness, and a sense of God's
call upon their lives, who nonetheless have
not been providentially utilized by God by
being placed in ministry of some sort. A
minority of them will have no giftedness either
– only desire. These are particularly pitiable.

In their minds, if they once ascended the sacred desk, the world would fall at their feet in awe of their spiritual ability. Anyone who has ever heard them teach or preach knows better. They, however, cannot be convinced otherwise. But for the rest, the need is to try to help them find some place of exercise. The problem is, they often will not accept any other place of service but pastoral ministry.

These are good, but wounded men. They can be very severe critics of preachers, teachers and ministries. However, they are often very correct in their criticisms. For this reason, they can be very valuable. Their own wounded pride makes them especially sensitive to pride in others. They can smell the stench of your own creeping sense of superiority a mile off. So they can be dear, dear friends of your ministry. They know how things SHOULD work, though have never done it themselves.

This is a hard group to utilize well, because giving them some sort of opportunity to minister often seems to be torture in and of itself. It is not where they believe they ought really to be. It's like letting them smell and chew the steak, but never letting them swallow. Pray often for these men. This is a very hard place to be in. And seek for much wisdom on their behalf. You will sometimes suffer great resentment from them, as they see God using your meager abilities, when their abilities, often genuinely superior to your own, seem ignored by God. They can also be some of your best encouragers.

j. *Prophets* – Specialists on the MIND OF GOD. The ones who have "heard from God" on almost every occasion. This group is driven by strong impressions and feelings. And they come in several different flavors. They can be difficult to distinguish from those with a genuine burden from God. But the ones who are being wrought upon by the Holy Spirit subject themselves to the Word of God, and are willing to roll up their sleeves and do the work behind the scenes. In contrast, these "Prophets" tend to be loose cannons. They can usually be spotted by the telltale sign that their "burden" is always about others – never about how they can serve. Or, if it is how they can serve, it is invariably as the leader. They want to make pronouncements.

Often, they may even be seeing a problem or an issue clearly, and really have some good insight. But their fear of not being listened to leads them to speak "prophetically" as a means of guaranteeing a hearing. And nothing, nothing but their view is in any wise accurate.

The biggest problem with these folks is that they tend to carry a sort of spiritual "air" about them that lends itself easily to getting a certain listenership. They are most often somewhat accomplished in some field, and thus are quite intelligent. Once someone is under their influence, the individual almost fears to cross or contradict them. They are great manipulators. Out of all the ones we've examined above, these are the least likely to be salvageable in terms of usefulness in the local assembly. Most often, they will not remain anywhere long where they are not afforded the platform or recognition they seek. They will suffer almost anything except being ignored. This they cannot abide. Being disciplined makes them martyrs. Being combated makes them legitimate. Being contradicted makes them furious. But being ignored makes them leave.

Three

The Complexion of Worship

---

2 Samuel 24:1: "Now again the anger of the LORD burned against Israel, and it incited David against them to say, 'Go, number Israel and Judah.' [2] The king said to Joab the commander of the army who was with him, 'Go about now through all the tribes of Israel, from Dan to Beersheba, and register the people, that I may know the number of the people.' [3] But Joab said to the king, 'Now may the LORD your God add to the people a hundred times as many as they are, while the eyes of my lord the king still see; but why does my lord the king delight in this thing?' [4] Nevertheless, the king's word prevailed against Joab and against the commanders of the army. So Joab and the commanders of the army went out from the presence of the king to register the people of Israel."

Every individual worship service has its own complexion. So it is, that any attempt to subjectively evaluate the power or effectiveness of your preaching in impacting your hearers' lives based upon your own "feelings" is almost invariably erroneous.

This is not to say that we are not conscious of God's Spirit working uniquely through us at times. George Whitefield was wont to refer to seasons when he preached with "great liberty." Martin Lloyd-Jones speaks of the "sacred anointing" and Spurgeon prefers the idea of "unction." Sometimes we are conscious of it – this unique manner in which the Holy Spirit makes His ministrations somehow palpable. Other times we are most certainly not conscious of it. But we must not use such intimations by the Spirit – or lack of them – as barometers by which we judge what is happening in the hearts of those to whom we are ministering. The danger here is manifold, because we can easily grow dependent upon such feelings.

When this happens, there are three common results. Just as David's numbering of the people was apt to plunge him into two great errors, so our subjective assessments will most often do the very same thing.

First, we find ourselves despairing if these feelings are not present. This is especially debilitating if the Father is pleased to withdraw such motions for any protracted period of time. We, like Timothy, are called to labor and be "instant" both in and out of season. What I feel like at any given time is not the measure either of the truth itself, nor of its work. A good chef can prepare succulent dishes even when his own nose may be stuffed up and he has no ability to smell the savory odors nor taste the dishes himself. Beethoven still composed and arranged brilliantly after losing his hearing. David was instructed not to number the people lest he see them to be few in number compared to his enemies, and hesitate to wage war as God might require. So it is with us. If we measure our preaching's fire power on the numbering and qualifying of our own chills, goose bumps, glory buzzes – or whatever else it is we think signals to us that God is at work - we will be timid, ill-prepared and faithless when such feelings are nowhere to be found. This is a sin against God. It is trusting our own sensual feedback over and above anchoring our faith in the God of the Word we are preaching. This is not to minimize our constant need to be seeking the Spirit of God to bless His Word abundantly as it goes forth. It is to keep us from using our mercurial emotions from being the test of what God is doing through His Word preached.

Second, just as we can flag in our resolve if we come to depend upon feelings that are suddenly not there, so we can just as errantly assure ourselves of great things when in fact we are woefully lacking – simply because the feelings ARE there. The second reason why David was not to number the people was so that he would not see how great his army was – and trust in that, rather than in God Himself. Once we have bought into the system of measuring things by these chills and thrills and ticks and shivers, we will plod on foolishly and to the detriment of the people, thinking God is greatly at work because we've got the "glow". Whether the glow was produced by our cold medicine or not seems irrelevant. And this, regardless of whether or not what we preached was even remotely biblical truth! This is exceedingly dangerous. Just because YOU thought you were on fire, doesn't mean the rest of the world wasn't aware you were just flaming out. Don't get me wrong, we should be preaching messages which impact us first, and at least as greatly as they impact our hearers. Encounters with the truth must move us, or we haven't really encountered the truth at all. But the measure of that movement – if it is just because we shed a tear or "felt" His presence or something else of the like – will lead us into deep and troubled waters. We will soon find ourselves both in our preparation and in our delivery seeking to evoke the same repetitive responses in us and in our hearers. We will aim at the feeling instead of at the truth which ought to inform and evoke the genuine feeling.

Third, if we court our own feelings in this regard, it should be of little surprise to us then that our hearers are doing the same. So it is, when you cease to deliver the goods – to give them the glory buzz any longer – they will do one of several things: either they will wonder what has happened to their spirituality ("Oh dear, the devil has been after me something fierce as of late"); or, they will wonder what has happened to yours ("Brother so-and-so has lost the anointing you know"). Still others will just start running after whatever and whoever can give them their candy back.

Fill them up with good food, and they'll have little room for the candy. Feed them on candy, and they'll just want something more chocolaty, sweeter, longer lasting and more gooey next time.

Four

Inappropriate Devotion

Proverbs 20:6: "Many a man proclaims his own loyalty, but who can find a trustworthy man?"

Men and women who profess love for you, your church or your ministry, who virtually know nothing more about it than the last time they visited there, are not your friends – at least not yet. They profess love to an unknown. Men and women who will swear love and allegiance too quickly and without knowledge will condemn and leave exactly the same way.

The point here is not to make you cynical, but simply aware of a very sad fact of life. Just as people run in and out of marriages too quickly, so the Church. It isn't that they are not genuinely impressed when they walk in. It isn't that their compliments and encouragements are not sincere when given. But they are gushed out without reflection and deep consideration. You can mark it down that such is always a sign of great immaturity. Young men and women think themselves deeply in love with those they have never met, but have only seen on television, in the movies or in magazines. If such continues when they age, they will rush into relationships of all kinds.

Typically, they will be unstable in their homes, their jobs and most other things they undertake. Filled with enormous enthusiasm at the start of everything, they will soon lose interest or be offended at some small point. Before long, they will be telling the pastor down the street (on their first visit) how they've been searching for a church and ministry like his for years. And at last they have found it.

What is worse is that these folks usually have some measure of talent or ability which could be of good use for the Body of Christ. However, their refusal to stay anywhere long enough to mature makes short work of every attempted project. If you take them in and use them as quickly as they have pledged their undying love to your congregation, you will just be looking for someone to take over their unfinished business before you know it. Surely this is one of the reasons why Paul admonished Timothy to "not lay hands on any man too hastily" (1 Tim. 5:22), and to let deacons be tested first (1 Tim. 3:10).

Maturity is unearthed in long term commitments carried out, not just sworn to. Many a promising start has ended with the words "I just didn't know what I was getting myself into." Though by far the most common comment upon exiting is: "I believe the Lord is calling me to something else."

Quite simply, you do not have the long hours to spare soothing the easily frazzled sensibilities of these knee-jerk responders. Such will steal valuable time from those in your flock who need real help, while you wrestle with how to keep this one happy and productive, who, by their accolades and pronouncements have led you to believe they will be your faithful and eternal partners in ministry. Let them attend faithfully for 18 months to two years, and then begin to hand them some responsibility. If they stick to it and discharge it well, you have found a good man or woman. If they need to be "needed" right away, you can be quite sure that they have come for the wrong reasons. They have come to have "their ministry." And when they cannot, they will leave, looking for some other "place of service," i.e. looking for some other place to be recognized.

Five

Mistaken Notions of Service

Luke 10:40: " But Martha was distracted with all her preparations; and she came up to Him and said, 'Lord, do You not care that my sister has left me to do all the serving alone? Then tell her to help me.' ⁴¹But the Lord answered and said to her, 'Martha, Martha, you are worried and bothered about so many things; ⁴²but only one thing is necessary, for Mary has chosen the good part, which shall not be taken away from her.'"

It is easy to substitute business or activity for spirituality. This is especially true in terms of studying God's Word and prayer. Praying is not studying and studying is not praying, and visiting the sick isn't either of them. All must be done, along with a thousand other things. None can be neglected. None can be confounded with the other, not safely.

What's worse, we can not only fall into this trap ourselves, we can communicate it to our congregations. It is a fiercely virulent strain of error. Soon, we have them thinking they cannot be spiritual unless they are in church – or engaged in some church activity – seven days a week. And as long as they are busy (read "committed") then we imagine that all is well with their spiritual lives. When all the while, the business we've concocted for them is the very thing that keeps them from time alone with God, and necessary time with their families.

There is a phrase which Spurgeon repeats often in his *Lectures to My Students*: "be much alone with God." In fact, all three of those books I mentioned above deal with the necessary duty of the minister keeping watch over his own soul. It is so very vital.

Let me just briefly reinforce this truth by way of a reminder. My dear fellow laborer, this reality cannot be stressed too much. Neglect of time alone with God is the single greatest spiritual pitfall you and I face. It has been true of every one of those who have gone before us, and it will be true for each who follows as long as Christ tarries. Much of this neglect is owing to an errant understanding of prayer, as though it is supposed to be a contest of verbal endurance – how long we can talk to God in an unbroken stream of non-stop chatter. Discouraged by our inability to simply spout off at God for hours on end, prayer will cease to be sought by us.

Let me say something which may seem a little strange to you on this count: prayer ought sometimes to be silent. Not simply without the uttering of words, but wordless itself. A space of time spent with the heart simply directed at God, knowing full well that He knows your needs better than you do, and that He is ready and able to meet them all. Waiting calmly in His presence, with the heart simply at rest before Him. Not trying to convince Him of anything. Not begging for anything. Not even confessing and repenting. Just waiting. Not with the antennae up either, as though to pick up heavenly and mysterious signals. But coming in before Him so certain of His grace and of His loving disposition toward us in Christ; so utterly convinced of His perfect care; so absolutely peaceful in the knowledge of His love and mercy – that nothing at all need be said. It is enough just to be there.

Prayer ultimately is fixing the whole of the soul's attention upon God. And this requires that we be alone with Him. If you spend no time alone with your spouse, your marriage will not only suffer, it will cease to be a marriage at all. The concept is two made one. If this is so humanly, how much more so spiritually.

No spiritual duty can be safely neglected and replaced with physical activity. Soon, we'll have nothing of substance to give our people. We must receive the broken bread from His hands before we can distribute it to them. Turn off the TV, the radio, the study tapes, the CD player, the computer, the cell phone and the pager – and be with God. Close the commentaries, the lexicons, the systematics, the biographies and the rest of the reference material – and be with God.

Be with God.

Be with God.

Six

Secret Travail

---

2 Corinthians 12:3: "And I know how such a man – whether in the body or apart from the body I do not know, God knows – ^{4} was caught up into Paradise and heard inexpressible words, which a man is not permitted to speak."

People do not have the slightest idea what it is you go through every week in delivering your soul in the pulpit – nor can they, nor should they. No one but a mother really knows what it is to give birth. Even among mothers, though they may compare notes regarding certain common experiences, still, the actual birth of any particular child is an experience wholly unique to that mother, at that time, in that place, under those circumstances. How odd it would be, if the mother afterward spent even an hour looking for commiseration regarding the birth – especially from the child! We would imagine her out of touch and strange. Yet the preacher will willfully enter upon the work of the ministry, and then expect those to whom he births the Word each week, to be all wrapped up in the details of the conception of it, the woes and cares of the gestational period, and the waxing and waning of every birth pang endured in the process of delivery. They do not care. They should not care. It is none of their business.

Your spouse will probably come the closest of any to knowing what it is you wrestle through each time, but even her knowledge must be limited. For the work we are about is born of an intimacy with God, a work of which it is vulgar to disclose to others.

The apostle Paul must be driven to extremes by the crisis in Corinth before he will begin to let them know the nature of his own struggles in the day-to-day woes he suffered for the sake of the ministry. Even at that, his litany of hardship in 2 Corinthians 11 is not meant to evoke pity, commiseration or reaffirmation from his readers. He is a most reluctant reporter of these matters. He considers each trial and tribulation on behalf of serving Christ a jewel of great value, not a bruise to be shown for the purpose of eliciting soft and comforting responses.

It is both a common and a deeply disturbing experience to leave the pulpit on any occasion, having poured out of the depths of your soul with all of the spiritual passion of which you are capable, and the exercise of every gift to the point of exhaustion, only to have the first person who approaches you drag you kicking and screaming into the realm of the mundane. After doing all you can to lift their vision toward Heaven and the Resurrected Christ, they spare no time telling you how strange it is that your nose whistles in perfect harmony with the low battery tone in their hearing aide. You have done all you can to make the glory of God a reality, and they want to know if YOU know you misspelled a word in your printed outline. You've crafted a biblically sound presentation of some great doctrine of eternal importance, and they say something like "but don't you feel that...?" as they present the diametric opposite – as though their two-second opinion formed after viewing half an episode of Oprah and reading an article in some obscure publication should counter the tide of 2000 years of orthodoxy. It is a heavy and oppressive grief to the soul to have that occur week in and week out. But! It is OUR grief, no one else's.

It is one of the sweet and peculiar sorrows we are allowed as ministers of the gospel, which grants us an experiential glimpse into the nature of what it must have been like for Jesus to minister on the earth every day. No one understood. No one really cared why He was there, nor could they. Even His closest intimates misunderstood His teaching. It was a designated part of His suffering that it be this way. For this is how it is with God and man on virtually every level. An amoebae has a clearer concept of nuclear physics than we have of God. Yet He lets us in on some of that in this unique way.

One last thought here – in our day of public obscenity, the notion of sacredness regarding almost anything is lost. 24 hours a day, you can turn on your radio or television, or pick up virtually any magazine, and be accosted with the most private details of people's lives and relationships which are no one else's business at all. There is no place among Christians for the locker room banter which rips the veil off the sanctity and privacy of the bedroom. But there should be even less of a place for us to expose to any other living creature the holy intimacies of our sacred times alone with God. Paul's experience of being caught up into the fourth heaven, was something he kept silent about for 14 years. And then, he only divulged it due to the extreme danger in Corinth. To want men to know of our secret wrestlings with God is as lewd as discussing the details of our lovemaking with our wives – with our office mates around the watercooler. It is obscene and offensive. It is a violation of the sacred. Let the sensationalists brag of their dreams and visions and their mystical experiences. God will deal with them after the manner of their sin. Such things are unseemly and degrading. Do not expect anyone else to ever enter into such matters with you. As Spurgeon said, (once again) "be much alone with God." But what goes on there is not for publication. How He deals personally and privately with your soul, and in preparation for your ministry, is akin to your inward parts being wrought in the womb. It is done quietly, sovereignly, secretly, and where no prying eyes ought to be. No one else can enter in. Do not let them.

Seven

Giving Versus Investing

---

1 Corinthians 9:16: "For if I preach the gospel, I have nothing to boast of, for I am under compulsion; for woe is me if I do not preach the gospel."

If you are giving with resentment, you have stopped giving and are begrudging the loss of return on your investment. As with our people, so with us – we often say "Oh that God would use me." But if He does, and MEN do not notice or thank us, we grow resentful. This is a sure sign that our giving isn't giving at all, but investing. And we are merely registering our displeasure with the rate of return on our investment. This is an extremely dangerous place to be. As one saint said long ago, it is one thing to be weary in the work, and quite another to be weary of it. Investors earning slender returns grow bitter.

The first warning sign of this sin is when we begin to resent the basic aspects of pastoral work. We will usually write this off to one of several other things, perhaps simple fatigue – which can indeed produce simple irritability. But the irritability of fatigue is not resentment against the work, as much as resentment that we do not have more time or energy FOR the work. This will be dealt with in another chapter below. What I am speaking of here is the sense that studying is an infringement, because nobody appreciates it anyway. Fatigue laments the inability to study more. Resentment has stopped serving to please God, but is now laboring to please self, which is fed only by men's responses. Fatigue blushes to receive compliments and is woeful that it cannot do more. Resentment almost refuses compliments altogether (in fake humility) and then secretly fumes that there were not enough compliments, from the right people, adequately expressed.

Dear brother, if this is you, you have become the "hireling" of John 10, and your concern is not how you can protect, lead and feed the sheep, but how you can benefit from them. You have stopped realizing that the flock is not yours, but someone else's. You want their wool for yourself. You will fleece them of the praise and honor that belongs to the Great Shepherd.

If this heart issue is not dealt with by confession and repentance, it will not be long before you will resent everything that surrounds your work. Everyone with a suggestion you will see as a power hungry challenger to your authority. No salary package will be sufficient. No amount of perks are really what you "deserve." You will treat people as though it is their job to serve you and your ministry, instead of your job to constantly labor for their loving sanctification before God. You will keep them as spiritual pygmies so that they need you, and at the same time resent them that they are spiritual babies crying for all your time.

None of this is to negate the fact that there are indeed some churches who abuse their pastors. Some are intentionally and cruelly treating their Shepherds both shamefully and wickedly. God will deal with such with a hard and heavy hand. But if you would see the model of one whose focus is clear and uncompromised in this regard, read Jonathan Edwards' sermon to his congregation AFTER he had been fired. He was deeply aware that not only will the people he served have to give an account of how they dealt with him, but of how he dealt with them. If our complaint to God is that the people have not repaid us well, He will remind us that we did not serve at their pleasure – but His. We were under-shepherds.

He is the Great Shepherd. The flock is His and so are we. Our ultimate argument is with what we perceive as His lack of gratitude for our labors, not theirs. We wanted some of His glory, and He was unwilling to share it with us.

Eight

Your Suffering Wife

Genesis 2:18: "Then the LORD God said, 'It is not good for the man to be alone; I will make him a helper suitable for him.'"

Genesis 3:16: "To the woman He said, 'I will greatly multiply Your pain in childbirth, In pain you will bring forth children; Yet your desire will be for your husband, And he will rule over you.'"

Your dear wife suffers far more from things said about or contrary to you than you can ever imagine – you must help her to remain sweet. Now I confess to you frankly, that I know more of the need here than I do of the solution. But some of it clearly rests in some things mentioned below.

Before we even get there, however, let me advance a word or two about choosing a mate. It may be moot to many of you, but for those young men contemplating the ministry who have not already found the blessed joy of marrying, please consider the following. It was Luther who said that three things make for a sound divine: tribulation, prayer and a good wife. He was spot-on. But let me add something. Never consider anyone for marriage (ESPECIALLY in light of ministerial aspirations) who does not manifest these three things: they must be your intellectual equal; your spiritual equal; and they must be kind. And if not your equal in these – your superior.

If you marry an unkind woman, you will afflict not only your own soul for years to come, but the soul of every one of those you seek to minister to throughout the exercise of your ministry. "It is better to live in a desert land than with a contentious and vexing woman" (Proverbs 21:19). "A constant dripping on a day of steady rain and a contentious woman are alike" (Proverbs 27:15). I warn every young couple seeking marriage very sternly in this regard. If you find that your potential spouse easily treats you coldly and unkindly in pressurized or stressful circumstances, run like the wind. It will only intensify a hundredfold later. A thousand fold if you are in the ministry. The like goes for you yourself. If you are not a kind person – if you find it easy to excoriate others, blame-shift under pressure or treat others unkindly when stressed – find another line of work. The ministry is not for you.

As to her intellect and spirituality, remember that when God made Eve, He made her a help MEET. In other words, one his equal to help him. If she is beneath you intellectually, you will grow frustrated with her at not having the capacity to challenge you at times when it is necessary. You will not be able to share with her the nature of your own thinking. Thus the very thing you are called to do for Christ will in fact cause a species of divide between you. This is terribly dangerous. You will find yourself unusually easy prey for the attentions of another woman later. The tired iron of "she doesn't understand me" will become a reality, and will render you unable to resist the charms of the one who comes along and can.

Before getting back to the main point of dealing with detractors, let me insert a word to wives here. Your husband the "minister" needs more of your tenderness toward him than he does of your hardness toward his detractors. Let me repeat that – your husband the "minister" needs more of your tenderness toward him than he does of your hardness toward his detractors. He will easily suffer their piercing attacks if he finds easy comfort and acceptance with you. Tend his wounds by pouring in the oil and wine of your love, while watching out for yourself lest you allow him to fall into self-pity. There is little more seductive and destructive than self-pity. Once fed, it has an insatiable appetite that will feed anywhere and any way that it can, blinding the eyes to real dangers of men and women alike who will take advantage of this state of mind for their own gain. Remember, he will soon begin to feed off your indignation to justify his own if this is left unchecked, and the two of you can hide behind a small fortress of isolation and bitterness. And bitterness defiles everyone who comes in contact with it. It will poison the very bread he tries to break and distribute from the pulpit each week.

A great lesson can be learned here from the prophecy of Simeon to Mary regarding Jesus. In Luke 2:35 that venerable saint says to Mary at the circumcision of her Son – "and a sword will pierce even your own soul—to the end that thoughts from many hearts may be revealed." I believe this verse should be read and contemplated by every dear woman who takes it upon her shoulders to be the wife of a minister of the gospel. For the day will come –

sooner, rather than later – when she will hear men and women alike speak of this her husband in terms that are not only unkind, but often untrue. Her desire is toward this man. She knows him as no one else possibly can. She is more aware of both his strengths and his weaknesses than even he himself is. And being given to him as he to her, just as surely as she has received him into her body – so even more into her heart, she cannot see him hurt or even attacked without feeling it within, and that with a double pain. For as surely as they are one, so the pain is just as much hers as it is his.

Let me suggest a few very simple directions for preventing some of the above. I'll not go into much detail on each. I believe the concepts speak well enough for themselves.

1 – We must be very careful not to let our wives defend us, as a way of being defended, while not defending ourselves. When this happens, we take solace that we are super-spiritual by refraining from self-defense, while the whole time we are leaping for joy inwardly at our wives' outrage over the offenses. It is as though we're too righteous to do it ourselves, but it's all right if THEY do it for us. It is a hypocritical trap. It is an excuse for sin. Beware.

2 - By praying together WITH them over those who are seeking to harm you. We will do almost anything else about our detractors, except the one thing we really need to do – pray for them. And it must be quickly pointed out that praying FOR them, and praying ABOUT them are not one and the same thing. We must beware that our prayers do not degenerate to the level of us merely gossiping to God about others. If they are truly Christians, and they are acting sinfully toward us, then our first desire needs to be seeing them freed from the sin that binds them. Yes, this is unnatural. We must apply to Christ for such a heart. But if He can pray "Father forgive them, for they know not what they do" from the cross, how much more we from the comfort of our living rooms? Yes, the sin will need to be addressed in the context of Church discipline as well. But it can never, under any circumstances, be the product of bitterness, revenge or a fleshly "tit-for-tat" pettiness.

3 - By probing them in conversation often to see how their attitudes are. Here, the husband and wife can minister to one another in a most magnificent way. And what a preventative it is from the bottling up of secret resentments.

Wives can do more for the good of congregations than can ever be told, if they will probe their husbands in the same way. But men, our wives love us, and seek to protect us. Because they naturally defend the home, they naturally defend us. Attacks upon us are attacks upon the whole family in their eyes and hearts. We must make it a priority to interact with them regularly over their attitudes toward those who may be of concern, so that they do not become burdened with the weight of unspoken and perhaps even unrealized griefs turned to resentment, or even resentment turned to hatred. It is a foul trap of the enemy and one which we must avoid at all costs.

4 - By teaching them didactically and by example what offering up imprecatory prayers is all about – lest we become spiritual vigilantes. My good friend Tracy Thieret in expounding Psalm 5 went very carefully through the wisdom of praying imprecatorily. Wisdom which when distilled ends in this – I am better off praying that God take vengeance upon my enemies than taking any other steps, for He will neither punish unjustly, overly, too little, with prejudice, nor neglectfully. We need to be able to turn these individuals over to Him.

5 - By developing a sound theology of suffering. Our generation knows very little of this. We have almost no room for suffering in modern theology at all. No suffering is to be tolerated, endured, worked through or received – let alone embraced. Yet Paul taught clearly that our suffering is to be sanctified for the good of the Body of Believers. The opening chapter of his second letter to the Corinthians is a straightforward call to learning the holy skill and joy of knowing that even in the deepest of trials, "Blessed be the God and Father of our Lord Jesus Christ, the Father of mercies and God of all comfort, who comforts us in all our affliction so that we will be able to comfort those who are in any affliction with the comfort with which we ourselves are comforted by God. For just as the sufferings of Christ are ours in abundance, so also our comfort is abundant through Christ. But if we are afflicted, it is for your comfort and salvation; or if we are comforted, it is for your comfort, which is effective in the patient enduring of the same sufferings which we also suffer" (2 Cor. 1:3-6). I wonder if many of us even remember that such passages are in our Bibles.

6 - By seeking comfort in one another often. How easily the wedge of disaffection can pry apart two made one in Christ, simply because we do not learn to go to one another for comfort. Men are especially guilty on this count. It is as though when God said "it is not good for man to dwell alone," He was simply adding an adornment to our lives instead of stating absolute truth. Lean on this woman God has given you. She is there for this purpose, and is complimented when you take her into your deepest confidence. Let her see you naked, and be unashamed before her. It is not a sign of weakness to need her so – it is a sign that you have learned something of her infinite value and God's glorious wisdom in giving her to you. She is much stronger than you realize, if you would let her be exercised in the right manner. And wives, you must do the same. This notion of sparing one another something by not confiding and trusting each other above all others is poppycock. Absolute rubbish! It will weaken your marriage and your ministry.

If you have a wife, she is a gift to you, and you to her. Learn to find true, sweet, understanding comfort in one another's arms, confidence, silence, conversation and trust – and a stranger will never come between you.

Forsake the fortress of your oneness, and you are both open and slow moving targets for the enemy of our souls.

Nine

The Exclusivity of Christ's Bride

———————————————————————

The apostle Paul delivers up an entire world of pastoral theology in *2 Corinthians 11:2. He writes: "For I am jealous for you with a godly jealousy; for I betrothed you to one husband, so that to Christ I might present you as a pure virgin."* With that I sound this warning: never fall in love with Christ's Bride – she is betrothed to another.

Paul was wrestling against the seductive and subversive super-apostles who were seeking to gain a place in the church that they might benefit by her. As he begins to demonstrate to his readers just how lewd these imposters are, he uses this one sentence simile, and in it articulates his philosophy of pastoral ministry.

The image is so simple and informative. The virgin bride is the church. The husband she is betrothed to is Christ Himself. And Paul? How does he think of himself in this? He is as though a close mutual friend of the bride and groom, the one who introduced them. And now the groom has gone away for a time – committing the care of His virgin bride to this friend, to keep her and protect her until He returns. Thus Paul sees these interlopers who are vying for her affection in Corinth – not as competitors to himself, but as trying to take liberties with the one he is sworn to keep until Christ returns.

I would submit to you that this is the very way that we as preachers and pastors are to consider our own relationship with the church. We may admire her beauty, delight in her company and revel in our usefulness to her – but she is not ours. We are guarding her virtue for Him. We have no right to fondle her, soil her garments or grow overly familiar with her. We are to direct her affections toward her intended, and to labor with all our might to keep her from inordinate affection for us, or anyone else.

Now the danger here occurs most commonly in four ways: you toward her; her toward you; outsiders toward her; and her toward outsiders.

You appeal to her, because you listen to her, and care for her. You are not shocked at her failures; encourage her when down-hearted; feed the need of her soul; comfort her in sorrow; and stand beside her in trials. And you share something of the qualities of her Betrothed. But you are not Him. At the same time, she appeals to you because she can offer you such affirmation, companionship and status. There is nothing quite so heady as when she adoringly lavishes praises on you for doing the very things you have been called by Him to do.

Others pursue her to rape her and steal her virtues for personal gain. They will seek to gain the advantage over her by telling her false doctrines designed to obscure Christ and His image. And she is drawn to them by those lies, and the promises of immediate and illicit fulfillment. Each and every one of these wrongly fostered affections must be turned to Christ. Oh that we would learn to have hearts of great propriety in our relationship to His beloved Bride. Nothing has so scandalized the Church over the centuries as this undue affection and liberty that has been allowed to grow between the Church and her pastors. It is the source of untold evils.

This, my fellow laborer, is another critical reason why Christocentric preaching is such an absolute must among us. Our job is to do everything in our power to lift up the divine charms and beauties of Christ so as to make her long for Him and Him alone: to continually remind her of the depth and power of His sacrificial love; to display before her His wonders and glories every chance we get; to speak well of Him always; to make her see His tenderness, His compassion, His strength, His faithfulness, His undying and limitless affection and the reality of His promises yet to be fulfilled. Make Him sweet to her again and again. Make her know how He has provided for all her needs until He returns. Make her to see that He will not suffer her to undergo any harm until He returns. Remind her of His wondrous forgiveness when she falls, and of the high nobility of His love which makes her a heavenly princess, though wrought of a lowly birth.

Like Abraham's servant, let us be quick to open the treasuries of our master, and parade the jewels of His devotion before Rebekah. Give her the gold ring and the bracelets for her wrists. Let her feel the weight and purity of His divine stores. Fill her with accounts of the loveliness and character of her intended. Woo her unto Him in such a way, that she cannot bear to think of lavishing her love upon any other. Make her deaf to the soft words of those who would seduce her by repeating the eternal words of Christ's great love to her over and over. Make her blind to their dazzlements by lifting up her eyes on high that she may behold Her beloved Jesus in all of His ineffable glory.

Make the touch of every other hand but His like sandpaper – letting her feel the nail scars in His palms often. Fill her rooms always with the sweet incense of His perpetual intercessions on her behalf, the perfume of His rich anointing and the oil of his gladness. Wash her garments often in the blood of the Lamb so that she neither grows accustomed to them being soiled, nor fails to be amazed at how brilliantly white He makes them. Make her to dine regularly at that table set only for Him and her, so that the taste and feel of His offering sustains her and spoils her for every other delicacy. Make her fall in love with Him over and over and over again. Spoil her for every other suitor – including yourself. Guard her virtue until the hour when He comes to make her His at last – and then you too will rejoice with joy unspeakable at that marriage supper.

Ten

Style Versus Substance

Matthew 23:27: "Woe to you, scribes and Pharisees, hypocrites! For you are like whitewashed tombs which on the outside appear beautiful, but inside they are full of dead men's bones and all uncleanness."

So you can talk well – well whoop dee do. So can every stand-up comedian, used car salesman, telemarketer and game show host. But style is no more a substitute for substance than looking at pictures of food can sustain your body. (OK, my sad attempt at sarcastic humor, but the plain truth is,) if we have nothing more to bring to the table than a glossy and well-choreographed presentation we've brought not one grain of good to anyone, and (quite possibly) done positive harm to many.

Never forget that the only thing we have to give our listeners is truth – and that not in general, but God's truth: saving, transforming, biblical, gospel truth. That blasphemous notion of days gone by that argued "all truth is God's truth," as though telling someone that $2 + 2 = 4$ has as much saving quality about it as the truth regarding Christ's substitutionary atonement, is still among us. It is simply dressed up these days in the glittering, putrefying rags of humanistic psychobabble, self-help Christianese and religious fadism. And it is endlessly spewed out of the clerical platitude factories of the spiritually bankrupt.

The "Talking Heads" of modern media have nothing on many of us. Our God-given faculty for speech and presentation has sometimes lulled us into being able to effortlessly and coolly handle Heaven and Hell (if we mention the latter at all) in the same sermon, and with the same silver tongued detachment they use when switching from the story about the 16 year old who brutally murdered his parents, to the next piece on baking Christmas cookies. If we have nothing more to give them than human opinions, foolish speculations and religious mumbo-jumbo, rather than what can impact their immortal souls for eternity, then we ought to sit down and let someone else speak who does. Beloved, this is not a game; not a show; not a contest to see who's the most polished, the slickest or the most capable. It is a divine charge to speak God's Word(s) to God's people, to declare the glories of our Christ and King, to call lost men to repentance and faith in Jesus Christ.

When a man is dying of a fatal disease, it is of little consequence (either to him, or in actuality) whether the remedy was transported in a vehicle with leather seats or cloth ones. It is the medicine that is of the utmost importance. When Lazarus lay dead in the tomb, do you think when he heard those words "Come forth!" that he cared for a single moment that Jesus wasn't wearing Armani; didn't arrive in a BMW; or that He didn't effect His speech and use soothing and colorful words to woo him out of the tomb? What utter nonsense. We will not stand before God and give an account of our ministries based on the marks we got from fallen men on how pleasing our elocution was. It won't matter one whit if we were multimedia savvy; facile with PowerPoint; could write a cool skit to illustrate our points; or had a Worship Team. The question will be: "Did you feed my sheep?" And we had better be able to show that we did so on the diet He proscribed.

Do not get me wrong here. This is no apology for ill-preparedness, unwillingness to study our craft of preaching, or to make excuses for dull, ponderous, clumsy or irritating verbal incompetence. But as Spurgeon said "nonsense spoken louder doesn't make any more sense." Nonsense spoken more eloquently or cleverly doesn't either.

When Luther was responding to Erasmus in *The Bondage of the Will*, he began by explaining why it had taken him so long to respond to Erasmus' little booklet. After stating simply that he found little in it worth responding to, he then wrote: "your book...struck me as so worthless and poor that my heart went out to you for having defiled your lovely, brilliant flow of language with such vile stuff. I thought it outrageous to convey material of so low a quality in the trappings of such rare eloquence; it is like using gold or silver dishes to carry garden rubbish or dung." I wonder how many of our sermons could be deserving of the same remarks. When once we begin to trade on our natural giftedness and make it a substitution for the communication of sound truth, we will soon make our hearers of all men, the most miserable.

W.G.T. Shedd addressed a group of seminary students in 1893 with these words: "We come, then, to the conclusion for which we have made these preliminary statements, namely, that in all Christian pulpits, however different may be the mental and oratorical characteristics of the preachers, the same kind of religious *impression* ought to be made and the same fundamental *truth* ought to be taught. The result of logical preaching, of imaginative preaching, of illustrative preaching, ought, with the divine blessing, to be the same. And what is the result? Plainly the conviction of men, if they ought to be convicted; their conversion, if they need to be converted; their sanctification, if they require it."

Eleven

Never Stop Learning

Proverbs 25:2: *"It is the glory of God to conceal a matter, But the glory of kings is to search out a matter."*

An academic degree is proof (we would hope) that one has completed a specific course of study in a given field. A degree (even an advanced degree) however, does NOT signify that one has learned all there is to learn, either in that field of study, or in general. Yet it is a tragic reality that many who have completed the necessary years of applied study which brought them their degree(s), cease the pursuit of knowledge in their field soon after they enter upon the practice of their profession. In a musician this is shameful. In a teacher, this is abhorrent. In a doctor it is deadly. In a preacher it is a crime against both God and man with eternal consequences.

There is no quicker way to guarantee that your preaching will be dull, repetitious and shallow than to be a man who has stopped learning. The single most neglected spiritual gift that God has given to man is gray matter. We are to use it and improve upon it in general, and especially in terms of God's Word. A facile mind is the greatest tool you and I have as preachers. And if it is not kept sharp by the application of it to ascertain more and more knowledge it will grow lethargic and worst of all – inbred.

If the only thoughts you are acquainted with are your own, you do not know how to think. Your thought process is stagnant, and the ideas it produces will be as brackish and unable to sustain life as the Dead Sea. If you never wrestle with contrary opinions, confront alternate views, think through difficult concepts, you will as surely atrophy intellectually as one who never exercises does physically. Your answers to the real questions of life which people face will become at best biblical platitudes, and at worst the brainless equivalent of "Because I said so."

Every generation faces crises of theology: attacks upon the authority, veracity, historicity, sufficiency and inspiration of the Scriptures; attacks upon the deity of Christ, the triunity of the Godhead, the person of the Holy Spirit and the nature of God; challenges to the notion of what the Church is; as well as regeneration, sanctification and glorification. In our own hour we are met with Openness Theism, New Perspective Theology, Hymenaen Preterism, Militant and Race based Reconstructionism, and the psychologizing of the Church – among others. And there will be countless new ones in the days to come. Some are nothing more than ancient perversions dressed up in new clothes. We need to constantly familiarize ourselves with how our forefathers in the faith faced those. Others are wholly unique. We are going to have to forge our own weapons in our day. Some the Church has refuted in the centuries gone by, and some it will have to rise up and meet anew. But it is we who preach and teach week in and week out who must be prepared to meet each and every one of those as they present themselves before us in the practical lives of those in our pews.

If we die intellectually, our people are sitting ducks. The unthinking priest of the Reformation era left his people in darkness and bound in sin. The unthinking Galatian walked right back into the waiting arms of the Judaizers. If we are unthinking men, what will we answer God when we stand before Him to give an account of how we kept the wolves at bay?

Now beyond the practical question of the rise of doctrinal issues in the venue above is the simple reality of our never ending quest to be filled up with the knowledge of God Himself.

There is no place where it is more true than in genuine theology, that you know nothing if you think you know anything. Anyone who spends time contemplating the infinite and comes away thinking he has comprehended more is a fool. He can only comprehend how little he knows. We will lose all sense of wonder, awe and transcendence if we stop our pursuit of Him. And if that be the case, how quickly will those who hear us begin to see the limits we have imposed upon God by our abandonment of the eternal exploration of Him?

Let me ask you – have you come to the end of God? Have you stopped contemplating the glorious infinitudes, the unsearchable riches, the unspeakable majesty and glory, the unfathomable wisdom and wonder of His inscrutable person and work? Does He cease to amaze you? Is His grace limited? His knowledge hedged in? His omniscience lacking? His omnipotence unable? His omnipresence merely biblical hyperbole? Then who and what do you have to preach but an idol of your own making? A God of your own construction. For in your personal cessation of the pursuit of God, you have found His limits, charted His form, become complacent with the image you imagined, and have, in the final analysis, robbed your flock of knowing God.

To stop learning, for the preacher, is to cease seeking after God. For we see (or we ought to see) in every field of inquiry new windows upon the glories and wonders of God. If you continue to learn, your people will be the beneficiaries. If you stop, they will suffer the consequences.

Twelve

Avoiding Controversy

Titus 3:9: "But avoid foolish controversies and genealogies and strife and disputes about the Law, for they are unprofitable and worthless."

Are you sometimes troubled at Jesus' somewhat enigmatic responses to questions He received? He was not trying to be obscure. He was sidestepping needless and fruitless controversies where nothing might be gained in the exchange. Where the point to be considered was important to His questioners and His disciples so that they might come to an understanding of the truth, He always discussed it. Where there were traps and useless wranglings over obscure and inconsequential debates, He sent them away with their heads spinning. He was laying down a principle for us: do your best to avoid controversy except in matters of God's truth, or clear biblical practice. But in order to do that, we need to understand both of the following skills: (1) do not answer a fool according to his folly, and (2) answer a fool according to his folly (Prov. 26:4, 5).

In the first injunction, we are being counseled to avoid falling into the "fool's" way of reasoning. It is no small weapon that the enemies of the gospel use which baits us into answering questions designed specifically to trap and discredit us – questions that have the appearance of profundity, when in actuality they are stupid, time-consuming and harmful.

Never allow yourself to be lured into the murky and nebulous regions of speculation that begin with the words: "what if?" "What if Adam had never sinned?" The foolishness behind this question should be apparent – it doesn't matter one whit! Adam DID sin. The question is – what is to be done about the fallen state of man! The endless arguments of supra-, sub-, trans- and infra-lapsarianism can quickly (and often do) degenerate into platforms for foolishness as well. We had best be about the business of mastering the revelation God HAS given unto us rather than trying to peer behind the curtain of what He has not.

When men get heated and divided over whether or not the forbidden fruit was a

pomegranate, a fig or an apple – it is best to
ask them if they have yet mastered the Lord's
words on sanctification or the epistolary sum
of the Pauline understanding of justification.
Good grief! What have we to do with such
nonsense when we have not yet risen to
devour the basics of Christian living? It is
worse than a group of toddlers who are just
learning to count arguing over the finer points
of quantum physics. If some fool wants to
waste your time asking you if God can make
a rock so big He cannot move it, ask him if he
is the man God made so stupid that he cannot
be saved? And would he know it if he was?
Men spring questions like traps. Do not
answer a fool by buying into his hypothetical
scenarios. Deal with the truth. Work with what
is, not what might be or could have been.
Gospel truth majors on reality, not
speculation.

On the other hand, we ARE to answer a fool
according to what his foolishness needs –
rectification. Do not be afraid to tell men they
are asking the wrong questions. Lost men are
blind, and many saved men still have blurry
vision. The more light we can offer, the better.
If a man asks how much he can still sin and
remain saved, you will not help him in the least
if you try to actually figure out some sort of

system of limitations. The question that NEEDS to be answered when one has tendered something like this is: how can a regenerate heart study to justify its sin so? Why he has asked the question itself always raises a far greater question. And if we will answer a fool as his folly requires, we must be ready to give answers to the questions they do not ask at all, but desperately need the answers for.

When such questions are in fact nothing less than thinly veiled litmus tests – be the most on your guard. Set your boundaries. Weigh carefully which issues you are willing to die for and which you are not. True Christian fellowship is not always bound up in the most exacting of terms on peripheral issues. Where we have unequivocal biblical truth, there can be no compromise of any kind. But where there is reasonable room for discussion, we must extend the brethren every possible liberty and avoid the divisiveness that is born of pettiness. Every man must delineate for himself (especially as a pastor) the lines he cannot cross on any given issue. But arrive at those decisions carefully, and with charity. There is no room for us ever to tolerate Pharisaical legalism. At the same time, we are not to be undiscerning imbeciles. Because we need to breathe does not mean we are required to inhale toxins.

Remember, sometimes, our brethren argue simply because they are weaker. Thus Paul's words to us in Romans 14:3 & 5-6 are especially wise: "The one who eats is not to regard with contempt the one who does not eat, and the one who does not eat is not to judge the one who eats, for God has accepted him." "One person regards one day above another, another regards every day alike. Each person must be fully convinced in his own mind. He who observes the day, observes it for the Lord, and he who eats, does so for the Lord, for he gives thanks to God; and he who eats not, for the Lord he does not eat, and gives thanks to God."

Thirteen

Sleep

1 Kings 19:5 : "He lay down and slept under a juniper tree; and behold, there was an angel touching him, and he said to him, 'Arise, eat'. [6] Then he looked and behold, there was at his head a bread cake baked on hot stones, and a jar of water. So he ate and drank and lay down again. [7] The angel of the LORD came again a second time and touched him and said, 'Arise, eat, because the journey is too great for you.' [8] So he arose and ate and drank, and went in the strength of that food forty days and forty nights to Horeb, the mountain of God."

In the immediate aftermath of Elijah's encounter upon Mt Carmel, one thing was abundantly clear – he was physically, emotionally and spiritually exhausted. As our text demonstrates above, when he got to lay down under that juniper tree, he slept. And such was his exhaustion that "he ate and drank and lay down again."

I dare say that many today would have considered him quite weak and unfit for service if he couldn't stand the rigors of his calling any better than that. Where was his faith? But Elijah, like you and like me, had his limits. And woe unto the man who does not know his, or has come to believe he must regularly try to live beyond them. He will live among the perpetually exhausted, and in the long run be quite unproductive for all his stress and strain.

Some men, like Wesley did, require little sleep. The problem is that Wesley demanded the same from his charges without regard for their individual and natural constitution. He thought men to be indolent and sinful if they complained of needing more than four to six hours of rest per night. Many a good man has fallen victim to the artificial constraints of another's habits, abilities or nature. Either they feel great guilt for not being able to keep the same pace as others, or ruin themselves trying to keep it. And it is all utter foolishness.

The average man (believe it or not) needs about eight hours of sleep per night as his regular portion. If you need less – God bless you as you redeem the extra hours you've been given. If you need more, may God grant you wisdom to use your narrower window of labor with the greatest productivity. But beloved, find what you need, and function within those parameters or you will invite trouble of all kinds.

In stark contrast to Wesley, I've read that J.C. Ryle confessed to needing large quantities of sleep just to function. Sometimes ten to twelve hours per night. No doubt, he may have had some undiagnosed physical condition which contributed to that. But all of us need what we need. Our individual constitution was given to us by Him. To do less than we need, will eventually be to give less than we can. There is no inherent virtue in exhaustion. God is not somehow more mysteriously glorified by your efforts because you go about them groggy, heavy eyed and weak. What strange logic it is which convinces us that unless we are at death's door, or at least stretched beyond human limits – we are less than spiritual – is beyond me. Personally, I am convinced it is a deception of the enemy.

We can have our own version of pastoral antinomianism in our quest to be spiritual men. You will remember those who Paul theorizes might respond to his teaching on grace by saying "let us sin that Christ might be glorified." Well, we can actually reason to ourselves that if God's strength is made glorious in our weakness, then we will do our best to make ourselves weak. Believe me, we have plenty of real weaknesses for Him to use to keep us humble and dependent upon Him, without foolishly manufacturing our own by neglect and wrong-headedness.

There is an amazing connection between a lack of physical rest and susceptibility to temptation to be considered here as well. Lower a man's natural resistance, and you have a foothold against his powers of reason and resolve. This is why brainwashing techniques often employ sleep deprivation. Keep a man always on the edge of exhaustion and he will do irrational and dangerous things. We are called to wield the Sword of the Spirit on a regular basis. If our senses are not kept sharp, our thoughts clear, our reasoning powers in good condition, we will preach error simply by virtue of the loss of being able to make the right distinctions we must in rightly dividing the Word of Truth. We will not be able to reason past our own errors in study. We will grow heavy in our delivery and light in content. Confusion will rule the day. Novelty will catch our eye quicker than truth, and the devil will find us easily led astray after subtle shades of perverted truth.

You owe both your God and your congregation your best powers. As one wag said, sometimes the most spiritual thing you can do in that regard, is to take a nap.

Fourteen

The Flagging Flock

---

2 Corinthians 11:24-30: "Five times I received from the Jews thirty-nine lashes. Three times I was beaten with rods, once I was stoned, three times I was shipwrecked, a night and a day I have spent in the deep. I have been on frequent journeys, in dangers from rivers, dangers from robbers, dangers from my countrymen, dangers from the Gentiles, dangers in the city, dangers in the wilderness, dangers on the sea, dangers among false brethren; I have been in labor and hardship, through many sleepless nights, in hunger and thirst, often without food, in cold and exposure. Apart from such external things, there is the daily pressure on me of concern for all the churches. Who is weak without my being weak? Who is led into sin without my intense concern? If I have to boast, I will boast of what pertains to my weakness."

Remember that many of the folks you minister to feel just as crummy as you do. This is by design. In fact, I am convinced that it is often the case that the pastor feels quite exactly as many under his charge do at any given time. As Christ shared in our suffering, so we are called to be "filling up what is lacking in Christ's afflictions" (Col. 1:24). We suffer much so that we might minister well. Unsympathetic counselors are no counselors at all. This is not to invite molly-coddling nor to allow indolence and sinful neglect of holy duties to go unchallenged; but it IS to have somewhat of an experiential knowledge of that which our hearers are facing. The common aggravations of everyday life which afflict you, afflict them. The tiredness and fatigue which sometimes threatens to engulf you, is this very week overwhelming some of those who will occupy the pew this Lord's Day. Berating them for not attending the midweek service will do no good whatever.

Moses' great error in smiting the rock when instructed by God to speak to it was twofold. First, he said "Listen now, you rebels; shall we bring forth water for you out of this rock?" (Numb. 20:10). Who is "we"? There is no "we" in bringing forth water out of a rock – there is only Him! When we insinuate ourselves into the equation, we have usurped God's own glory, and such will not go unpunished. But secondly, Moses was angry with them when God was not. James warns us that "the anger of man does not achieve the righteousness of God" (Jas. 1:20). And when we fail to take into account the nature of what the ravages of sin, the world and the enemy have wrought upon and within those to whom we minister week in and week out, our preaching and our counsel will be unnecessarily harsh, unfeeling, uncompassionate and hard. William Gurnall wrote: "It is not the least of a minister's care and skill in dividing the Word, so to press the Christian's duty, as not to oppress his spirit with the weight of it, by laying it on the creature's own shoulders, and not the Lord's strength."

It is true, that "we do not have a high priest who cannot sympathize with our weaknesses, but One who has been tempted in all things as we are, yet without sin" (Heb. 4:15). We should remember then, that we too as ministers have been appointed to suffer with our people that we might sympathize with their weaknesses. It is fitting, in seasons of our own temptations and trials, to assume that if we are being set upon in some unique fashion, it is because at least one, if not more,

under our care are being set upon at the same
time and in the same manner. And so we
should use this as a special, providential
impetus to prayer.

Are things difficult between you and your
wife this week? Have your children offered
more than their usual challenges? Have your
finances been suddenly strained? Is your own
mood and countenance inexplicably downcast
or heavy? Have you been robbed of sound
sleep? Have aches and pains distracted you
from your normal course? Has it been days
since your mind has focused easily upon the
tasks at hand? Has weariness broken your
resolve in some area? Have you found that
you have been neglecting the secret duties of
true holiness? Is the Word suddenly dull and
difficult? Have past sins been invading your
mind, and remorse over them been stealing
your peace in Christ? If so, dear brother, then
it is for certain that any and all of these have
been affecting your flock as well. Know it
when you enter the sacred desk – and do not
scold where the Balm of Gilead needs to be
applied. Pray for them. And above all, minister
unto them the comfort your Lord and God
has used to comfort your own soul in those
same dark hours. Every discomfort you have,
and more, afflict everyone of those who will

hear you break the Bread of Life to them this next Lord's Day. As you have had to look to Christ and the sweet Comforter whom He sends, so direct them to the same Fountain whilst remembering that their thirst burns as hotly as your own.

Fifteen

Ministry is Not About You

Romans 11:36: "For from Him and through Him and to Him are all things. To Him be the glory forever. Amen."

I would call your attention to Jesus dealing with Peter in the latter part of John 21. Whatever else may be drawn from this incident between Jesus and Peter in John, this much is true: Jesus uses very specific language with a threefold emphasis. But it is the personal pronoun in each of the charges that I wish to call to your attention here. Feed MY sheep; shepherd MY lambs; tend MY flock. Just as we are to be constantly reminding our hearers that the world does not revolve around them, so we must be doubly diligent to remind ourselves that ministry is not all about us. Everything is about Him. We are His. The Church is His. The ministry is His. He allows us the unspeakable honor of laboring with

Him – though we are nothing in ourselves. We bring nothing to the table in ministry. The gifts and callings are just that, gifts and callings. They are neither natural proclivities nor natural inclinations. It is the Spirit that works in every child of God both to will and to do of His good pleasure, and that is not one whit different with ministers.

It would be good for all of us to dwell upon the first chapter of Ephesians regularly and with deep reflection. This glorious passage opens to the mind the threefold reality in everything. Salvation is of God, by God and for God. He made us for Himself. He redeemed us for Himself. Whenever we forget this central theme, it will not be long before an unnatural possessiveness crowds into our souls, which when unrequited (as it is right it should not be) we begin to grow bitter and frustrated with those we are sent to nourish, cherish and protect.

When I was a young man, I remember a pastor who had long regarded my Dad as his mentor in the ministry, coming by the house to discuss the crises his church was embroiled in. After he left, my Dad simply shook his head and said: "The real problem with his church was on his own lips the entire conversation – it was MY church, MY ministry, MY people,

MY vision, etc. Everything was about him."
Nothing was about Christ.

My dear brother, we have but one message,
one Lord, one faith, one baptism and one
purpose. "All things by Him, all things for
Him, all things through Him." If His glory is
not greater in your pursuit than your glory,
recognition, acceptance or comfort – flee the
pulpit today. There is nothing but disaster
ahead. We let passages like Luke 17:10 easily
tumble off our lips when we speak to others,
but we need to truly hear and digest these
words for ourselves: after having done all, we
are to remember that we are but unprofitable
servants.

At the risk of sounding a tad extreme or
novel, let me just try to drive this home to
you the simplest way I know how:
It's not about you.
It's not about you.
It's not about YOU!

The ministry never has and never will be
about those of us who minister, but it is ever
and always all about Him.

Sixteen

The Superintendent of the Church

John 14:16: "I will ask the Father, and He will give you another Helper, that He may be with you forever."

One of the most damaging concepts to enter the Church throughout the centuries since Jesus' Ascension is this cock-eyed foolishness that Christ left the Church in the hands of men when he departed. This is both the seedbed of popery, self-appointed apostles and self-ordained institutionalism of all kinds. Jesus appointed no human successor(s), arranged no institutional polity, nor left the door open for others to assume the position at their own or anyone else's whim. This is of the utmost importance lest we imagine ourselves to have some sort of personal authority among men. Our only authority is God's Word. If it is anything else, it is imagined.

Now to be utterly clear on this matter, we need to look briefly at Jesus' preparatory words to His disciples throughout those closing days of His earthly ministrations. With all of His discussions regarding His being taken and killed, the prophecies of the destruction of the Temple and of His return – He also included the necessary information that He would not leave them comfortless, but would send another Comforter in His place. Thus, they would not see Him, but He would be with them. The simple reality is, that He sent the Holy Spirit to administrate the Church, and let them know that He would be with them forever. This is why there is no See of Peter. This is why there can be no other prophets who arise in His room. This reality immediately disqualifies every self-appointed and anointed figurehead over the body of Christ from Sun Myung Moon to the Pope. The Spirit is the one given, and He continues with us until Christ returns. So it is that everyone who assumes the role of under-Shepherd within the Body of Christ must do so only in as much as he is controlled by the Spirit of Christ who is never self-promoting, never hungry for power, never lording authority over men, and serves only as a servant to Christ and His loved ones.

Just as the Spirit never speaks of Himself, but takes what is Christ's and makes that ours, so we – if we are under His auspices – will not make anything of our ministries, but will take what is Christ's and magnify that, and live according to the Spirit of holiness.

We must be continually wary of any who would elevate themselves by thinking to speak as the head of the Church in any capacity globally, nationally, regionally or locally, and that includes ourselves.

Above all of this, if we do not labor with this in mind, we will constantly be trying to do the work which belongs to the Spirit alone. We may preach the Word so that men are convicted by the Spirit when confronted with the truth, but it is not OUR job to convict men – it is His. If we take up the task, we will drive them into the ground and destroy them. He alone has the power to convince the mind of sin, and of Christ's righteousness, and of the coming judgment. If we forget that, we will try to do those things when we cannot – will try either to strong arm them by our "authority," or faint due to our inability to be effectual. If we labor under His auspices – we may preach and teach with the utmost confidence that the Word will have its desired effect, and labor under a light burden, and an easy yoke.

Seventeen

God's Seasons

---

*Ecclesiastes 3:1:"There is an appointed time
for everything. And there is a time for every
event under heaven."*
*1Corinthians 3:6 : "I planted, Apollos
watered, but God was causing the growth."*

There is perhaps no greater source of
confusion and discouragement in
ministry than in our lack of discerning God's
ordinary method of operation in terms of
seasons. We are wrongly given to want
extraordinary seasons of refreshing and
visitation to be the norm, just as we are prone
to consider seasons of dryness and little fruit
as permanent conditions. Both are errors of
the same root. Neither accounts for the
observable phenomena which we experience
every calendar year in nature. There are
winters, springs, summers and falls. In some
places, those might be seen rather as rainy

seasons, dry seasons, etc. But that God ordinarily administrates His physical universe in some measure of seasonal ebb and flow should instruct us in some measure. This is so that we do not expect a harvest at the same time as we sow, nor neglect to water what has been sown because in our discontent we try planting again.

These things are true personally, in the life of a local Church, perhaps regionally, nationally or even globally. But the point is this – we need to discern that God is working out His purpose and plan, even when the season is other than the one we prefer.

Now in terms of this affecting us personally, let me speak to you about the nature of your own spiritual life. You are not always cognitively the same at all times. There are seasons when the heart is warmer and more inclined toward a sensitivity (if you will) regarding spiritual matters. And there are times when you personally will be dry and arid. These are seasons of the soul. It is not to say that God does not sometimes draw our attention to Himself through days of straightness or trial. He does. But it is to say that these are typically seasons – not singular events. As Paul counseled Timothy to be "instant" both in and out of season – so we must learn the habits of constancy which suffice in those changing times. Yet we must be careful not to regard them over much lest we magnify them beyond their ordinary course. We can become distracted and defeated if the moment we do not experientially enjoy the sense of His presence, we go looking for direct causes. They are often not available. Job's wasn't. Sometimes we do know that we are suffering the hand of His faithful chastening. I believe that James is clear, when chastening is the cause, confession and repentance is the cure. But here we are speaking not of direct causes, but of seasons. What seem to be inexplicable times of nearness and withdrawing, fruitfulness and barrenness, these we are to expect, and to remain constant in them.

Notice too, that such seasons affect those who are in our churches. Often, a family will undergo an extended period of time of difficulty and trial. Then, almost as soon as it came, it begins to lift. This is God's hand. These are His seasons. We must seek Him in these hours, and not look at circumstances as either omens or conclusions. God is at work. He wants us to draw near to Him in every season. He is moving in and through the providential arrangements of our lives. And in each He is always looking to have us look to

Him: to learn to walk with Him regardless; to trust Him no matter what; to believe Him rather than to try and read the "signs"; to rest in Him and His unchangeable promises rather than to look to techniques, programs and fixes.

About two years after I came to pastor the Church where I now am, God was pleased to begin to open the doors and send us many new faces – some churched, some un-churched, some from similar backgrounds, some not. But as the growth began to be quite noticeable, some began to inquire as to what it was we were doing. Certainly, there were some changes from the previous pastors. But were those changes to be credited with what was happening? No. Soberly and carefully, we needed to look back and recall that this Church had a long history. The founding pastor had planted for many years. He saw many come and go. He saw the complexion of the Church change over time – times of plenty, times of less. After his retirement, my own father came to pastor here and for nearly twenty years labored in the same field, watering and tending, he enjoyed seasons of harvest and seasons of dryness too. And so it is that I happen to be here during a season of harvest. I get to enjoy the fruit of nearly sixty years of other's labors. But neither the founding pastor sowed in vain, nor did my dad water in vain, but God ultimately gave an increase. Make no mistake – it is simply God's increase, in God's time. There is no formula. There is no secret. There is faithfulness to God in His seasons.

I do not know where these words will find you today, dear brother. Perhaps you have been laboring long and have seen little for your efforts. You have been breaking up the fallow ground, and you have found it exceedingly hard and dry. The plowing has been difficult, for the natural tendency of the soil is to remain undisturbed. The seed has gone in, but you cannot see any growth yet. All around you are the long furrows of your labor, but there is so little fruit – hardly enough to sustain you. Do not be discouraged. It is not His season of harvest, but all the seasons are His. Apply yourself to the work in the hour in which you find yourself. His Word does not return void.

Perhaps you are in the midst of great harvest, so that you can barely contain it. Do not be puffed up with pride as though you had done it. Do not sit down and catalogue your great innovations as though they are the reason why. For if it is only your techniques, then it is not God and these will fade as quickly as they came.

But if it is God, you have nothing to boast in. Pray that God equips you to do the work necessary in the hour in which you find yourself. And take time to bless those who planted and watered so faithfully before.

Or maybe you are in between. You can see the heads popping up, but they are not ready to be plucked yet. There is green, and hope, but the growing season seems so long. Tend to the weeds. Fertilize the field. Keep the water flowing. God's season for harvest is yet ahead. You may not be the one there to bring it in. In your own seasons, you may be moved to other labors. But know well that your labor for Him is never in vain. Wait His time. Wait His seasons. Adjust your labors to match the time. God will honor His Word.

Please note that this is an important dynamic to recognize in the basic life of a Church as well. There are days of visitation, days of expectancy, days of rejoicing, and days of fasting and mourning. Never require of God that Pentecost last longer than its time, nor refuse it when it is at hand. Our need to make everything God has ever done into a perpetual requirement for every congregation in every age is most damaging. What ought to be normative must be dictated by the common teaching of the Scripture, not the record of extraordinary events. At the same time, we cannot cast in concrete a theology that attempts to bar God from acting extraordinarily when and where He wishes. We must leave room for seasons of revival, reformation and visitation, as much as we must not artificially try to produce, harness or imitate them.

Let us cry for rain. And when He gives it, let us make the most of it. But when it is gone, let us look to Him again as we busy ourselves in the intervening seasons, rather than trying to erect sprinklers so that we can pretend it's raining or fool others into thinking it is. The disciples had to learn to be more pleased with the promised Spirit, than with Christ's bodily presence after three and a half years. May we learn to do the same. May we recognize that whatever the season, it is sent by His hand – and therewith to be content.

Eighteen

Laugh

Proverbs 17:22: "A joyful heart is good medicine, But a broken spirit dries up the bones."

No one else in the world has anything to laugh about but Christians. That is not license to be flippant, giddy or foolish. It is to remember that (as Spurgeon said) "we work as though it all depends upon us, but pray knowing that it all depends upon Him." So we breathe deeply, we sit back, and we laugh.

Whoever pits the gravity of our task against the joy of knowing that we labor in Christ's power, under His promise and by the Spirit of His presence, has brought a false dilemma. The question is not: should a pastor be grave, or rejoicing? But "how do we do both?"

If you have no doctrine of sovereign grace – rooted in God's eternal election, you will labor with much frustration and fear. Joy will escape you as you see people sin their lives to hell. YOU could have kept back if only you had the key, the magic phrase, the right strategy, technique, approach or program. Hogwash. Preaching is both the savor of life unto life, and death unto death. The death does not diminish our joy, but rather our joy overcomes the death. Do not get me wrong, this is not resignation to being complacent about men perishing into a Christless eternity. Indeed, it is nothing of the kind. But it is to rightly discern that it is Christ who saves, not us, and that there will be no empty place settings at the marriage supper of the Lamb. It is to be confident that our preaching will be the Word which does not return unto Him void, because it is His designated means to bring in the elect.

Never forget as well that we live in the constant loving care of our Sovereign God. If we as God's preachers are as bound up in the anxieties of the world – AS the world – how shall we ever teach our people to live in the joy and confidence of Christ's great supply? Let me ask you, how are YOU doing with the problem of anxiety? If you cannot trust Christ, how can you ask others to? If you cannot trust Christ for the needs of every-day life, then how dare you ask other men to trust Him with their eternal souls? Are you convinced of your reconciliation to the Father by the finished work of Christ at Calvary? Then why are you living as though your acceptance is based upon performance? Do you preach Christ or works? And if you preach Christ, then why do you look and sound as though you still have not received either the pardon or the promises that attend to being His?

Even when we mourn, we do not mourn as the world does. They have no hope. Ours is a life infused with hope in every single aspect of it. Even our failures are redeemed unto Him. "For I am convinced that neither death, nor life, nor angels, nor principalities, nor things present, nor things to come, nor powers, nor height, nor depth, nor any other created thing, will be able to separate us from the love of God, which is in Christ Jesus our Lord" (Rom. 8:38-39).

There is probably no greater contradiction in terms than to conceive of a joyless Christian. And little more so reeks of artificial piety (versus the genuine) as prune faced, joyless, bitter, unapproachable, grouchy sourpusses who act as though they never once heard that the gospel is good news.

Just a short while ago I was away speaking at a conference. After a season of getting to know the other speakers and enjoying some particularly sweet fellowship together, one of the men said something incredibly profound: "It's so nice to meet some Calvinists, who aren't angry about it." His words were so accurate. If there is any group of people anywhere who should be living confidently, securely, joyfully and sweetly, it is those who best know the glorious fullness and wonder of serving a God who is truly Lord over all. What a disgrace to the name of Christ are men and women who claim to know that their sins are forgiven; that the wrath justly due them has been poured out upon Christ; that His righteousness is imputed to the; and that the surety of all His promises is incontrovertibly sealed in His resurrection – who then act as if being miserable was a virtue.

Richard Baxter wrote on this subject this way: "I desire the dejected Christian to consider, that by his heavy and uncomfortable life, he seemeth to the world to accuse God and His service, as if he openly called Him a rigorous, hard, unacceptable Master, and His work a sad unpleasant thing. I know this is not your thoughts: I know it is yourselves, and not God and His service that offendeth you; and that you walk heavily not because you are holy, but because you fear you are not holy, and because you are no more holy....if you see a servant always sad, that was wont to be merry while he served another master, will you not think that he hath a master that displeaseth him?…You are born and new born for God's honor; and will you thus dishonor Him before the world? What do you (in their eyes) but dispraise Him by your very countenance and carriage?"

Let us never forget that while the Kingdom of God is not meat and drink – it most surely IS righteousness (His imputed to us – so you can skip the performance anxiety), peace (we have peace with God through the shed blood of Jesus Christ) and joy (did you get that? JOY), in the Holy Spirit. O how blessed we are! O how little we revel in it! Shame on us!

Learn a good joke. Learn to tell it. Not to be clever, or the hit of some party, but so that you do not forget how to laugh. There will be no tears in Heaven, only unalloyed joy. We're not there yet, but we can and should have a foretaste.

Nineteen

Spiritual Temperatures

Proverbs 27:23: "Know well the condition of your flocks, And pay attention to your herds."

The Puritan Richard Baxter had some problems of his own, but when it came to dealing directly with the souls of those under his charge, he was without peer. Laboring in the field at Kidderminster, he was disposed to visiting and catechizing every family in his church with astounding regularity. It has also been reported that he conducted a brief spiritual "interview" (if you will) with each one under his charge yearly, if at all possible. The interview was quite simple, but extremely effective.

Baxter's interview process went something like this. First, Baxter would ask: "have you grown in Christ in the past 12 months?" If the answer was "yes", then the follow-up question was: "what are your evidences for believing so?" If, however, the answer was

"no", then Baxter's query was – "why not?"
Now the value of such direct and pointed
questions should be immediately obvious to
us. In such a case, you are asking the
individual to speak directly to the condition
of their own soul before God. This is both
good for them to survey, and for you to be
able to work with them accordingly.
Remember, you are doing so as one who must
give an account of this one before the throne
of God. It is a loving and healthy pursuit.

All that being said, I might suggest to you
that there is a means of ascertaining similar
information on an ongoing basis – virtually
without notice if you are willing to take the
time, and leave yourself open to some probing.
It is all wrapped up in this - listen carefully to
the questions people ask you.

If those you minister to are asking the same
questions over and over again, then they are
stuck. As they mature, their questions mature.
And the general rule that I have noticed is
that they begin mostly asking "how to"
questions. They want lists of do's and don'ts.
But as they progress under the systematic
teaching and preaching of God's Word, they
move more to questions of principle, and
doctrinal clarity.

When children are quite small, their whole frame of reference is bound up in two basic words, yes and no. At first, they are told not to touch this or that. It is enough that they learn the "what" before they learn the "why". But if they never progress to being able to operate on the "why", there is a serious problem. The more mature a person becomes, the less they operate on simple directives, and the more they operate upon principles and complete outlooks. The questions you are asked from week to week will reveal these things if you are paying attention.

We have found it helpful to actually have one night a month which is Q & A night. They can come with their Bible questions, questions about something they may have read, heard or seen, and are especially encouraged to ask about anything that has been preached or taught in our pulpit or classes. Baxter in fact took one night a week where people could come to his home if they had questions about his last Lord's Day sermon. If they know they CAN ask, they will. And those questions will be a treasure-trove of spiritual information for you to glean from. You will know what books they are reading, what television shows they are watching, movies they are seeing, what other preachers and teachers they are drawing from, and where their hearts stumble and need help. You will also be able to fill in the gaps where preaching cannot go. We have but limited time in the pulpit each week. We cannot possibly address all of the truth we need to, nor especially help them apply it in their individual and varied circumstances. Being open and available to deal with questions on a regular basis will prevent the need for all sorts of extra seminars, etc, which are born mostly out of people's sense of not knowing how to apply the biblical truths they have heard. It will also tell you whether or not you are communicating the truth clearly in your preaching and teaching. It's a make-up exam for every sermon.

Twenty

Leading is Going

Deuteronomy 31:7: "Then Moses called to Joshua and said to him in the sight of all Israel, 'Be strong and courageous, for you shall go with this people into the land which the LORD has sworn to their fathers to give them, and you shall give it to them as an inheritance. [8] The LORD is the one who goes ahead of you; He will be with you. He will not fail you or forsake you. Do not fear or be dismayed.'"

You cannot lead anyone anywhere you yourself are unwilling to go. So it is that the spiritual depth of a congregation will never exceed that of its leadership. If you are complaining over the spiritual immaturity of your own flock, look to yourself first – especially if you have labored among them a long time. Have you been growing? What are you reading? What are you doing for the health and growth of your own soul? Are you looking to mortify your own lusts? Is the prayer closet being neglected? Is the Word studied only for what you can teach out of it? I know these are hard questions my friend, but they are so necessary.

I might add here that while it is not an inviolable rule that a congregation's lack of spiritual growth is always tied to the leadership – it is certainly the general rule. There are some exceptions. There are cases where good, godly and faithful men have labored conscientiously and carefully and still the people have virtually refused to grow. Environment isn't everything. If it were so (as mentioned above), Adam would never have fallen. Jesus was the best exemplar of a pastor that can be found. He is the "Great Shepherd." But He still had Judas in His ranks.

In Revelation 2, the Lord commends the Ephesians' deeds, toil, perseverance, and their acute testing and weeding out of false apostles. Nor had they grown weary in their labors. But they surely had left their first love, and the chastening hand of God was being outstretched to remove their lampstand – perhaps their pastor – because of their condition. Sometimes a Moses does get an obstinate people. However, more often than not, the people and the pastor share a similar level of passion.

Moses could only lead the people out of Egypt because he was willing to leave there himself. Joshua could only lead them into Canaan in as much as he was willing to stop wandering in the wilderness. If you are still entangled in the world, is it any surprise that those who listen to you are too? If you are still wandering around in the wilderness – looking for manna falling from Heaven when you should be getting ready to plant the first crops in Canaan – is it odd then that those who have been feeding where you have taken them to graze are looking for that too? Is it any wonder that they do not chase out the inhabitants of the land and prosecute the battle against their own indwelling sins, if you have long since made treaty with your own?

As leaders in Christ's Kingdom, we cannot be mere signposts pointing the way, but we must be Shepherds who lead them along the paths of righteousness for His name's sake. We must be walking the path ahead of them, clearing the way of the stumblingblocks and with an eye out always for the wolves. We must lead if we would have them follow. We must be willing to go ourselves, wherever it is we

want them to go. We must be advancing toward
Heaven personally.

If we want our people to grow in grace and
in the knowledge of the Lord, then dear
brother, we must be ever about the same
thing. It is so easy for us to confuse the
impartation of theoretical truth with genuine
leadership. This is not a "do as I say, but not
as I do" proposition. We must walk before
them to identify, clear out and warn about
potential dangers. We must walk with them
to help navigate the dark and twisting path.
We must walk behind them lest the enemy
rise up when we are unaware and tear at their
souls while we contemplate the rising sun
ahead.

Christ's leadership meant being in the boat
with them while it was being swamped – even
if asleep for a moment – or coming to them
when not aboard, getting aboard, and getting
them to shore. It meant asking them how they
thought the need of the multitude should be
met, then demonstrating to them how it really
should be done. It was giving them clear
instruction, and being there to pick up the
pieces when they couldn't cast the demon out
of the boy themselves. It meant letting them
listen to the way He dealt with detractors and
seekers alike, showing them how to conduct

themselves at secular affairs by actually going to the wedding Himself. We know He wept beside the tomb of Lazarus, because they saw Him and heard Him.

Leadership in Christ's Church means living Christ both in and out of the Church. And we cannot take them one single step beyond the line we are unwilling to cross. So let us lead them to Him, as we take up our crosses and follow too.

Post Script

Once near the end of a sermon I heard John MacArthur bring things to a close by quipping: "I've already told you more than I know." In some ways that captures my own actual feelings at the close of this little book. No one is an "expert" on pastoral ministry, least of all me. It is Christ who is the Good Shepherd. Indeed, He is the "Great Shepherd of the sheep" as the writer to the Hebrews puts it; and the Chief Shepherd in Peter's words. And we would be remiss if, together in the midst of our labors, we ever let that triple reality slip. For in it, we are reminded that we are not under-shepherds left to ourselves or to our own devices, but still under His own watchful, glorious shepherding.

Dear brother laborer, never forget that He does not neglect to shepherd your soul even while you are tending the portion of the Flock He assigned to you. Repair to Him often. Seek His counsel constantly. Bring your personal needs to Him daily, as much as you bring those under your care. Look to the ministrations of His Spirit in leading, feeding and protecting your own soul even as you seek to be of use doing the same for your charge. He who keeps us never slumbers and never sleeps. He is ever watching for us, that we may sweetly, comfortably and confidently labor. We might fail, but He never will. And He takes the ultimate responsibility for ALL His own to bring them safely home – you and those you minister to. Trust Him. Trust Him with your own soul as well as with theirs.

"All that the Father gives Me will come to Me, and the one who comes to Me I will certainly not cast out. For I have come down from heaven, not to do My own will, but the will of Him who sent Me. This is the will of Him who sent Me, that of all that He has given Me I lose nothing, but raise it up on the last day. "For this is the will of My Father, that everyone who beholds the Son and believes in Him will have eternal life, and I Myself will raise him up on the last day." Even we pastors.

Reformation & Revival Ministries

Reformation & Revival Ministries, in partnership with Christian Focus Publications, has an imprint line of books for the purpose of providing resources for the reformation of the Christian church through the life and work of Christian leaders. Our goal is to publish and distribute new works of pastoral and theological substance aimed at reforming the leadership, life and vision of the church around the world.

Reformation & Revival Ministries was incorporated in 1991, through the labors of John H. Armstrong, a pastor for the previous twenty-one years, to serve the church as an educational and evangelistic resource. The desire from the beginning has been to encourage doctrinal and ethical reformation joined with informed prayer for spiritual awakening. The foundational convictions of the ministry can be summarized in the great truths of the sixteenth century Protestant Reformation and evangelical revivals of the 18th & 19th centuries.

To accomplish this vision the ministry publishes a quarterly journal, *Reformation & Revival Journal,* designed for pastors and serious readers of theology and church renewal. A more popular magazine, *Viewpoint,* is published six times a year. The ministry also has an extensive array of books and tapes.

Dr. Armstrong speaks in conferences, local churches and various ministerial groups across the United States and abroad. The ministry has a no debt policy and is financed only by the gifts of interested people. The policy from the beginning has been to never ask for funds through solicitation, believing that God provides as he will, where he will, and when he will. An office and support staff operate the ministry in suburban Chicago.

Further information on the ministry and resources can be found at -

Reformation & Revival Ministries
P. O. Box 88216
Carol Stream, Illinois 60188
(630) 980-1810, Tel
(630) 980-1820, Fax
E-mail: RRMinistry@aol.com   Web: www.randr.org

Christian Focus Publications

We publish books for all ages. Our mission statement -

STAYING FAITHFUL

In dependence upon God we seek to help make his
infallible word, the Bible, relevant. Our aim is to ensure
that the Lord Jesus Christ is presented as the only hope
to obtain forgiveness of sin, live a useful life and look
forward to heaven with him.

REACHING OUT

Christ's last command requires us to reach out to our
world with his gospel. We seek to help fulfil that by
publishing books that point people towards Jesus and for
them to develop a Christ-like maturity. We aim to equip
all levels of readers for life, work, ministry and mission.

Books in our adult range are published in three imprints.

Christian Focus contains popular works including
biographies, commentaries, basic doctrine, and Christian
living. Our children's books are also published in this
imprint.
Christian Heritage contains classic writings from the past.
Mentor focuses on books written at a level suitable for
Bible College and seminary students, pastors, and other
serious readers; the imprint includes commentaries,
doctrinal studies, examination of current issues, and
church history.

For a free catalogue of all our titles, please write to:
Christian Focus Publications, Ltd
Geanies House, Fearn,
Ross-shire, IV20 1TW, Scotland,
United Kingdom
info@christianfocus.com

For details of our titles visit us on our website
www.christianfocus.com